CARE STANDARDS ACT 2000

EXPLANATORY NOTES

INTRODUCTION

1.   These explanatory notes relate to the Care Standards Act 2000. They have been prepared by the Department of Health, with assistance from the Wales Office and Department for Education and Employment, in order to assist the reader in understanding the Act. They do not form part of the Act and have not been endorsed by Parliament.

2.   The notes need to be read in conjunction with the Act. They are not intended to be a comprehensive description of the Act, so where a section or part of a section does not seem to require any comment, none is given.

SUMMARY

3.   In November 1998 and March 1999, the Government published two White Papers on its proposals for social services in England and Wales. Detailed proposals for the regulation of private and voluntary healthcare in England and for the regulation and inspection of social care and healthcare services in Wales were set out in consultation documents issued in 1999. The Government's proposals for the regulation of early years education and day care were set out in a consultation document issued in 1998. The recommendations and proposals for the Children's Commissioner for Wales were set out in Sir Ronald Waterhouse's Report *Lost in Care*, and in the report of the Health and Social Services Committee of the National Assembly for Wales on a Children's Commissioner. This Act implements the main proposals in these documents that require primary legislation

4.   The relevant documents are listed below –

- *Modernising Social Services (Cm 4169)*, published in November 1998
- *Building for the Future (Cm 4051)*, published in March 1999
- *Regulating Private and Voluntary Healthcare: A Consultation Document*, published in England in June 1999
- *Regulation and Inspection of Social and Health Care Services in Wales – A Commission for Care Standards in Wales*, published in July 1999

- *Regulating Private and Voluntary Healthcare in Wales*, published in August 1999
- *The Regulation of Early Years Education and Day Care*, published in March 1998
- *Review of the Regulation of Early Years Education and Day Care in Wales*, published in August 1998.

- *Lost in care – The Report of the Tribunal of Inquiry into the abuse of children in care in the former county council areas of Gwynedd and Clwyd since 1974*, published in February 2000. (HC 201; ISBN 0-10-556660-8)

5.   In summary this Act -

- establishes a new, independent regulatory body for social care and private and voluntary healthcare services ("care services") in England to be known as the National Care Standards Commission;
- provides for an arm of the National Assembly for Wales to be the regulatory body for such services in Wales;
- establishes new, independent Councils to register social care workers, set standards in social care work and regulate the education and training of social workers in England and Wales;
- establishes an office of the Children's Commissioner for Wales;
- reforms the regulation of childminders and day care provision for young children;
- provides for the Secretary of State to maintain a list of individuals who are considered unsuitable to work with vulnerable adults.

6.   The main purpose of the Act is to reform the regulatory system for care services in England and Wales. Care services range from residential care homes and nursing homes, children's homes, domiciliary care agencies, fostering agencies and voluntary adoption agencies through to private and voluntary healthcare services (including private hospitals and clinics and private primary care premises). For the first time, local authorities will be required to meet the same standards as independent sector providers.

7.   In England the Act provides for an independent National Care Standards Commission to undertake this regulatory function. In Wales this function will be carried out by a new arm of the National Assembly for Wales, which will be established as either a department or an agency of the National Assembly for Wales.

8.   These new arrangements will replace those set out in the Registered Homes Act 1984 (which will be repealed in its entirety) and those provisions in the Children Act 1989 which deal with the regulation of voluntary children's homes and registered children's homes. Community homes will now be regulated. The regulation of voluntary adoption societies will come under the umbrella of the new arrangements. Local authority fostering and adoption services will be subject to inspection, as will the welfare arrangements in all boarding schools and further education colleges which accommodate children.

9.   The Act provides for the regulation of the social care workforce, by establishing a General Social Care Council (GSCC) for England, and a Care Council for Wales (CCW), to be known in Welsh as Cyngor Gofal Cymru. These Councils will regulate the training of social workers and raise standards in social care through codes of conduct and practice and through other means. For the first time a register of social care staff will be set up and maintained by each of the Councils. The Act makes provision for the abolition of the Central Council for Education and Training in Social Work (CCETSW), which currently regulates training in social work throughout the UK.

10.   The Act establishes an office of the Children's Commissioner for Wales and sets out its functions and powers, which will extend to all the services for children regulated in Wales under the Act: children's homes, residential family centres, local authority fostering and adoption services, fostering agencies, voluntary adoption agencies, domiciliary care, the welfare aspects of daycare and childminding services for all children under the age of eight; and the welfare of children living away from home in boarding schools. The Commissioner's powers and functions include the review and monitoring of arrangements for dealing with complaints, 'whistleblowing' and advocacy; the examination of particular cases; and providing assistance, including financial, to a child in making a complaint or in other proceedings. These powers will also extend to children receiving services in other settings regulated under this Act, such as private hospitals.

11.   Arrangements for the regulation of child minding and day care provision for young children will also be reformed. Responsibility for the regulatory function in England will transfer from local authorities to Her Majesty's Chief Inspector of Schools for England (HMCIS) under a new arm of Ofsted. This new arm will bring together the regulation of childcare and early years education. In Wales, these functions will transfer to the new regulatory body for care services to be established as part of the National Assembly for Wales. Early years education in Wales will continue to be inspected by Her Majesty's Chief Inspector of Education and Training in Wales, through Estyn (the Welsh equivalent of Ofsted). Under the revised arrangements in both England and Wales, regulation will be carried out to new national standards. In addition, those working with or coming into contact with older children will be required to demonstrate that they are suitable to do so.

12.   The Act imposes a duty on the Secretary of State to maintain a list of individuals who are considered unsuitable to work with vulnerable adults. A single list will be established for both England and Wales. It will operate in a similar way to the list established under the Protection of Children Act 1999. Specified care providers (care homes and domiciliary care agencies which must register with either the National Care Standards Commission or the National Assembly for Wales, and prescribed services within the NHS and independent health sector), and employment agencies and businesses which provide or supply individuals to work in care positions, will be under a duty to refer people to the list in certain circumstances. Care providers will also have to carry out checks of the list before offering employment to potential recruits in a care position working with vulnerable adults, and to refuse employment in such a position to any person included in the list. Provision is also made for registration

authorities to make referrals to the list, and for referrals to be made as a result of certain inquiries.

13.   The Act provides for a right of appeal against the decisions of the new regulatory authorities and Councils established under the Act, decisions of HMCIS in England in connection with the regulation of child minding and day care and decisions of the Secretary of State regarding the vulnerable adults protection list.   Appeals will lie to the Tribunal established under the Protection of Children Act 1999 (which will cover both England and Wales).

14.   Other provisions in the Act include –

- changes to the regulation of nurses agencies in England and Wales, removing the nurses agencies' exemption from the Employment Agencies Act 1973, and repealing the Nurses Agencies Act 1957. Nurses agencies will also be required to register with the National Care Standards Commission or the National Assembly for Wales;

- Before Part II of the Act comes fully into force, the Children Act 1989 will be amended to remove the exemption on the requirement to register in the case of small private children's homes (which provide care and accommodation for fewer than 4 children). Such homes will be registered by local authorities until responsibility passes to the National Care Standards Commission and National Assembly for Wales;

- the Registered Homes Act 1984 is to be amended to require the registration under Part II of that Act of all dentists' premises where wholly private dental treatment of patients under general anaesthesia is carried out. This will take effect for the period that the Registered Homes Act remains in operation, until it is replaced by the commencement of the relevant provisions of this Act. Responsibility for the registration of such premises will then pass from the Health Authority to the National Care Standards Commission and the National Assembly for Wales;

- amendments are made to the Protection of Children Act 1999 to modify its application to employment businesses and to extend the scope of the Act to cover persons disqualified from working in independent schools on the grounds of their unsuitability to work with children.   Further provision is made for persons to be referred to the list kept under that Act by the National Care Standards Commission or the National Assembly for Wales, or following the result of an inquiry.

- The Local Authority Social Services Act 1970 ("LASS Act") is amended, adding to Schedule 1 of that Act a reference to Section 17 of the Health and Social Services and Social Security Adjudications Act 1983 ("HASSASSA Act"). The effect of this is to allow the provisions of the LASS Act (for example powers of statutory guidance and direction under Section 7) to apply to local authorities' functions under Section 17 of the HASSASSA Act. Those functions relate to charges levied by local authorities for non-residential social services.

BACKGROUND

15.   This section provides a brief description of the current legislative framework for the regulation, registration and inspection of the care services covered by this Act.   The two principal pieces of current legislation concerned with residential care are the Registered Homes Act 1984 and the Children Act 1989.   For more detail about the legislation see Annex 1 to these Notes.

The Registered Homes Act 1984

16.   The Registered Homes Act 1984 covers independent residential care homes, nursing homes and mental nursing homes and private hospitals. Residential care homes, which provide residential accommodation with both board and personal care (but not nursing or mental nursing care) are registered under Part I.   Homes which provide nursing or mental nursing care are registered under Part II.   The definition of nursing home in Part II embraces a wide spectrum of provision from traditional nursing homes and mental nursing homes through to clinics, acute hospitals and psychiatric hospitals. There are exemptions from the requirement to register.   Exemptions include children's homes as defined in the Children Act 1989, NHS hospitals and residential homes provided by local authorities under Part III of the National Assistance Act 1948.   Homes may be dually registered under Parts I and II.

The Children Act 1989

17.   The Children Act provides for three types of children's home: community homes (which include controlled and assisted community homes), voluntary homes and registered homes:

> • *Community homes* (Part VI of the Children Act) are provided by, or partly financed by, local authorities.   Homes provided and financed by local authorities are known as maintained community homes. Homes provided by a voluntary organisation and partly funded by local authorities are known as controlled or assisted community homes. Community homes are not required to register but are inspected by local authorities.

> • *Voluntary homes* (Part VII of the Children Act) are provided by charities or other not-for-profit organisations (voluntary organisations).   They are regulated by the Secretary of State.

> • *Registered Children's Homes* (Part VIII of the Children Act) are provided by private individuals or companies for profit.   They are registered by the local authority. Small private children's homes which accommodate fewer than four children, are not required to register at present and are not inspected.

Other Relevant Legislation

18.   Other services covered by this Act are provided for either in these Acts or other legislation. Local authorities provide fostering and adoption services under the Children Act 1989 and the Adoption Act 1976 respectively. Nurses agencies are subject to the Nurses Agencies Act 1957. Matters relating to the regulation of training for social workers are dealt with under the HASSASSA Act.

19.   Legislation relating to child minding and day care provision in England and Wales is set out in Part X of the Children Act 1989, which places a duty on local authorities to keep a register of childminders and day care providers, and to require providers to meet reasonable standards. The legislation governing nursery education inspections is in the School Standards and Framework Act 1998, and applies to both England and Wales.

20.   The Protection of Children Act 1999 provides for the Secretary of State to maintain a list of persons unsuitable to work with children. Childcare organisations are required in certain circumstances to refer individuals for inclusion on the list, and to check whether an individual is included on the list before offering them work in a child care position. They are prohibited from taking the person on if he is listed. An independent tribunal is established by section 9 to hear appeals against inclusion on the list. The Act amends Part V of the Police Act 1997 to allow information about inclusion on the list to be available where appropriate from the Criminal Records Bureau (CRB) as part of a criminal record certificate or an enhanced criminal record certificate. Until such time as the CRB takes on its functions under Part V of the Police Act 1997, those who must make inquiries under the Act about the inclusion or otherwise of an individual in the list will be entitled to the information from the Secretary of State.

THE ACT

21.   The Act is in nine Parts:

    • **Part I** provides for the establishment of the National Care Standards Commission in England and establishes the National Assembly for Wales as the equivalent registration authority in Wales. Part I also contains definitions for the purposes of the Act;

    • **Part II** makes provision for the regulatory procedures to be followed by the National Care Standards Commission in England and the National Assembly for Wales. The Secretary of State and National Assembly for Wales are given powers to make regulations in relation to the care services regulated under this Part of the Act and to issue national minimum standards applicable to all the services to which the registration authorities and providers must have regard;

- **Part III** provides for the inspection of local authority fostering and adoption services by the National Care Standards Commission and the National Assembly for Wales;

- **Part IV** concerns the functions of, and procedures to be followed by the General Social Care Council and the Care Council for Wales;

- **Part V** provides for the establishment of an independent Children's Commissioner in Wales;

- **Part VI** provides for the regulation of child minding and day care services for young children and provides for checks on the suitability of persons working with older children;

- **Part VII** imposes a duty on the Secretary of State to maintain a list of individuals who are considered unsuitable to work with vulnerable adults, and makes amendments to the Protection of Children Act 1999;

- **Part VIII** makes provision about children in boarding schools and further education colleges and makes new arrangements for the regulation of nurses agencies; and for statutory guidance on local authority charges for home care services; and

- **Part IX** contains supplementary provisions.

COMMENTARY ON SECTIONS

22.   Throughout the Act, sections have been drafted such that they apply to both England and Wales where possible. Unless otherwise stated, in these notes, references to functions or duties of the registration authority should be taken as referring in England to the National Care Standards Commission ("the Commission") and, when applied to Wales, be taken as referring to the equivalent functions or duties of the National Assembly for Wales. "The Council" means in England the General Social Care Council and in Wales the Care Council for Wales. The "appropriate Minister" means the Secretary of State in relation to England and the National Assembly for Wales in relation to Wales.

PART I INTRODUCTORY

23.   **Part I** sets out definitions of establishments *etc* and other terms for the purposes of the Act. *Section 6* establishes the National Care Standards Commission ("the Commission") as the registration authority in England. *Section 7* sets out general duties of the Commission, which include monitoring the provision and quality of registered social care services, informing and advising the Secretary of State, supporting consumers through the provision of information, and encouraging the development of better services. *Section 5* identifies the National Assembly for Wales as the equivalent registration authority in Wales, and *section 8* makes equivalent provision for its general duties in respect of its functions under Part II.

Preliminary

24.   *Sections 1-4* define the services which are to be regulated by the registration authorities. The services are children's homes, independent hospitals, clinics and medical agencies, care homes, residential family centres, domiciliary care agencies, nurses agencies, fostering agencies and voluntary adoption agencies.

Section 1 Children's homes
25.   *Subsection (2)* defines a children's home as an establishment which provides care and accommodation wholly or mainly for children. This will catch community homes, voluntary homes and registered children's homes (including small private children's homes) as defined in the Children Act 1989, and homes for disabled children. *Subsection (3)* excludes a place where a child is cared for by his parents, a relative, a person with parental responsibility for him or a foster parent. *Subsection (4)* excludes NHS hospitals, independent hospitals and clinics, schools and other institutions and gives the appropriate Minister the power to make other exceptions in regulations. It is intended that regulations will be made to except, for

example, homes where children take holidays or certain hostels set up by professionals to accommodate apprentices (such as footballers or jockeys). *Subsection (6)* provides that any school which provides accommodation for more than 295 days a year for any individual child must register also as a children's home. *Subsection (7)* clarifies the definition of foster parent for the purposes of this section.

26.   Small private children's homes, accommodating fewer than four children, are not required to register under the Children Act 1989. However, *section 40* amends the Children Act to require the registration of such homes by local authorities in the interim.

Section 2 Independent hospitals etc.
27.   *Section 2* sets out the range of independent healthcare services which are to be regulated. *Subsection (2)* excludes NHS hospitals from the definition of independent hospitals and clinics.

28.   *Subsection (3)* defines an independent hospital as any establishment which has as its main purpose the provision of psychiatric or medical treatment for illness or mental disorder (including palliative care) or which provides one or more of the services listed in *subsection (7)* ("listed services"), and any other establishment which provides treatment for people liable to be detained under the provisions of the Mental Health Act 1983. *Subsection (6)* provides that the definition of "people liable to be detained" does not include people who are on leave granted under section 17 of that Act. This definition of "independent hospital" will encompass all those hospitals and mental nursing homes registered to take detained patients which are currently regulated under Part II of the Registered Homes Act 1984 and other private or voluntary hospitals which are currently not regulated – for example those run by bodies established by Royal Charter or by special Act of Parliament.

29.   *Subsection (4)* defines an independent clinic as a prescribed type of establishment (other than a hospital) where medical practitioners provide services (including services which are provided for the purpose of an independent clinic otherwise than on the clinic's premises, for example in a patient's home). The definition excludes an establishment in which medical practitioners provide NHS services. This will bring private primary care premises, where prescribed, within the regulatory framework for the first time.

30.   *Subsection (5)* defines an independent medical agency as an undertaking (which is not an independent clinic) which consists of or includes the provision of services for private patients by medical practitioners. It excludes any agency that provides NHS services. This will bring wholly private GP call-out services within the regulatory framework.

31.   Premises in which "listed services" are provided come within the definition of a hospital. *Subsection (7)* defines the listed services as medical treatment under anaesthesia or sedation, dental treatment under general anaesthesia, obstetric services and medical services in connection with childbirth, termination of pregnancies or cosmetic surgery. The category of dental treatment under anaesthesia will, by means of regulations, apply to wholly private

dentistry only, and NHS arrangements will be changed so that comparable requirements apply to both public and private sector dentistry. It also provides for the appropriate Minister to specify other treatments involving the use of prescribed techniques or technologies. These would be treatments which pose a particular risk to patients. For example, at present regulations made under the Registered Homes Act 1984 prescribe treatment with Class 3B and Class 4 lasers as such treatment.

32. *Subsection (8)* gives the appropriate Minister power to make regulations excepting establishments from the requirement to be regulated and to amend the list of "listed services" by adding or removing services.

Section 3 Care homes

33. *Section 3* defines a care home as any home which provides accommodation together with nursing or personal care for any person who is or has been ill (including mental disorder), is disabled or infirm, or who has a past or present dependence on drugs or alcohol. The definition is intended to include residential care homes and nursing homes, as defined in the 1984 Act. The Commission will be able to impose conditions on care homes as to the categories of person they can accommodate. Residential care homes run by NHS bodies will be required to be registered under this definition of care homes as the provision of residential (as against nursing) homes is not a core NHS function as such. Local authority provision under Part III of the National Assistance Act 1948 will be required to be registered.

34. "Personal care" in the context of care homes includes assistance with bodily functions where such assistance is required. This may include, for instance, assistance with bathing, dressing and eating for people who are unable to do these things without help – see *section 121(9)*. This means that an establishment is not defined as a care home unless that type of assistance is provided where required.

35. *Subsection (3)* excludes NHS hospitals and private hospitals and clinics, including establishments which receive patients liable to be detained under the Mental Health Act 1983 (see paragraph 28 above), and gives the appropriate Minister power to make other exceptions in regulations. (Homes which take patients on section 17 leave under the 1983 Act but do not take detained patients will need to be registered as a care home not as a hospital).

36. Homes which provide personal care and accommodation for disabled children are to be treated as children's homes and not care homes.

Section 4 Other basic definitions

37. *Subsection (2)* defines residential family centres. Such centres undertake monitoring and/or an assessment of parenting capacity on a residential basis where there is concern that parents may be unable to respond appropriately to the needs of their children. This could include specific accommodation for teenage mothers and their babies. They may be operated by local authorities, voluntary organisations or private agencies. At present they are not

regulated, but in future all residential family centres will be required to register with the registration authority.

38.   *Subsection (3)* defines domiciliary care agencies. These agencies supply staff who provide personal care for people in their own homes. The definition encompasses any agency that arranges the provision of personal care for people who need assistance by reason of illness, infirmity or disability. Individual care workers are not included unless they themselves carry on or manage the agency.

39.   *Subsection (4)* defines fostering agencies. The definition is intended to include both independent agencies which provide a fostering agency service to local authorities, and voluntary organisations (such as Barnardos) who operate in their own right. Both types of fostering agency recruit and train foster parents and place children with them. Agencies defined by *subsection (4)(a)* make placements under powers delegated to them by local authorities, and they may or may not be voluntary organisations. Agencies defined by *subsection (4)(b)* are voluntary organisations which place children with foster parents in their own right.

40.   *Subsection (5)* defines nurses agencies. These will now be subject to registration by the Commission. In addition, the Nurses Agencies Act 1957 will be repealed, and nurses agencies will also be subject to the provisions of the Employment Agencies Act 1973 (see notes to *section 111*).

41.   *Subsection (7)* defines a voluntary adoption agency as an adoption society within the meaning of the Adoption Act 1976, which is a voluntary organisation. An "adoption society" is defined in that Act as a body of persons whose functions consist of or include making arrangements for adoption.

Registration authorities

Sections 5 and 6 and Schedule 1 Registration authorities
42.   These sections establish the National Care Standards Commission as the registration authority in England, and the registration authority in Wales, which is to be established as either a department or an executive agency of the National Assembly for Wales.

Section 6   National Care Standards Commission
43.   *Section 6* establishes the National Care Standards Commission. It is a statutory body corporate, which will exercise in England the functions conferred upon it by or under this Act or other legislation.   The constitutional arrangements and general provisions for the Commission are set out in *Schedule 1*, which makes provision for the Commission, the General Social Care Council and the Care Council for Wales (see notes on *section 54* below).

44.   *Subsection (2)* provides that the Commission must, in the exercise of its functions, act in accordance with directions given to it by, and under the general guidance of, the Secretary of State. *Subsection (4)* provides that the power for the Secretary of State to issue directions, includes directions in connection with organisational and structural matters, such as, for instance, the establishment of regional offices, or a separate division for private and voluntary healthcare.

45.   The Commission will be responsible for the regulation of the whole range of care services from care homes for the elderly, children's homes, domiciliary care, fostering and adoption agencies through to independent hospitals, clinics, medical agencies and nurses agencies. It will also inspect boarding schools, further education colleges which provide accommodation and local authority fostering and adoption services. It will take on the regulation and inspection functions that are currently split between local authorities, Health Authorities and the Department of Health centrally. Some services will be regulated for the first time – these include local authorities' own care homes and children's homes and domiciliary care agencies.

46.   Under the provisions of *Schedule 1* the Commission (subject to directions) may take any necessary or expedient action to fulfil its statutory duties (*paragraph 3*). The Secretary of State has powers to make regulations governing the procedures of the Commission, and the appointment of members (*paragraph 6)* and for the appointment of a chief officer (*paragraph 8)*. The first chief officer will be appointed by the Secretary of State. The Commission will appoint subsequent chief officers itself, subject to the approval of Secretary of State. The following paragraphs are worthy of additional comment:

47.   *Paragraph 9*: The Secretary of State will be able to direct the Commission to appoint regional directors. In line with the White Paper, *Modernising Social Services,* it is intended that these regions will be based upon the regions of the NHS Executive.

48.   *Paragraph 10* provides that the Commission must appoint a member of staff as a children's rights director, whose role will be prescribed in regulations. The intention is that he should ensure that the work of the Commission in regulating children's services takes full account of children's rights and welfare. *Paragraph 11* provides that the Commission must appoint a director of private and voluntary healthcare, who will be a member of staff with functions to be prescribed in regulations. The intention is that s/he will preside over a separate healthcare division within the Commission, and will oversee the Commission's interests in, and responsibilities for, the regulation of independent healthcare.

49.   *Paragraph 12* makes provision for an authority to appoint staff and provides that an authority may pay or make provision for the payment of pensions, allowances, gratuities or compensation, subject to directions from the Secretary of State.

50.   *Paragraph 13* provides that the Commission may arrange for any of its functions to be carried out by a committee or member of staff of the Commission, or by another person.

Paragraph 14 makes provision to enable staff from other bodies, such as Health Authorities and the Commission for Health Improvement, to be placed at the disposal of the Commission and *vice versa*.

51.   *Paragraph 15* provides that the Commission may run conferences, seminars and other training events. *Paragraph 17* allows the Commission to charge a reasonable fee for non-regulatory activities. Although registration and annual fees will cover the costs of regulation, there are some activities which the Commission will carry out which it would not be fair to expect all registered services to pay for. The Commission might, for example, wish to charge a fee to those who attend its training events, in order to recover its outlay.

Section 7   General duties of the Commission
52.   *Section 7* sets out the general duties of the Commission, and therefore applies only to England. The duties in *subsections (1) to (7)* relate to services that are subject to regulation under Part II, with the exception of private and voluntary healthcare. These services are collectively known as "Part II services". The duties include monitoring the availability and quality of such services, supporting consumers through the provision of information and encouraging the development of better services.

53.   *Subsection (1)* provides that the Commission must keep the Secretary of State informed as to the provision, availability and quality of Part II services. This will include reporting on trends in the provision of long term care. *Subsection (2)* provides that the Commission will have the general duty of encouraging improvements in the quality of Part II services. It will do this by, for example, disseminating examples of good practice and giving advice to providers on how to meet the national minimum standards (see *section 23*). Under *subsection (3)* the Commission is required to provide information about Part II services to the public. This might include information about the location and types of services available, as well as the results of its inspections of individual providers. *Subsection (4)* provides that the Secretary of State may require advice or information from the Commission about any aspect of the provision of Part II services. *Subsection (5)* enables the Commission to advise the Secretary of State about changes to the national minimum standards with a view to seeking improvement in the quality of services. *Subsection (6)* provides for the Secretary of State to make regulations conferring additional functions on the Commission.

Section 8   General functions of the Assembly
54.   This section makes similar provision for the Assembly, as section 7 makes for the Commission. *Subsection (1)* sets out the general duties of the Assembly in relation to Part II services to encourage improvement in quality of services. *Subsection (2)* provides that the Assembly shall make information available to the public about Part II services. *Subsection (3)* provides a parallel power to that in section 7(6) so that the Assembly may, by regulations, confer additional functions on itself, but only where that function has already been conferred on the Commission by the Secretary of State. *Subsection (4)* provides for the Assembly to have powers to charge for fees in connection with its regulatory duties. *Subsection (5)* provides for the Assembly to provide training in relation to the attainment of national

standards. Equivalent powers for the Commission are in *Schedule 1*, which does not apply to the Assembly.

Section 9 Co-operative working

55.   This section gives the Secretary of State a power to introduce regulations enabling the Commission (or the Assembly) and the Commission for Health Improvement (CHI) to delegate functions to one another. It recognises that, although their roles are distinct (CHI is a key part of the arrangements for modernising the NHS and will review the arrangements that NHS organisations have in place to update and improve the services they deliver; in contrast, the Commission will seek to ensure the individual independent healthcare providers have safeguards and quality assurance systems in place by regulating them against set national minimum standards), they also have common interests. For instance, CHI's review of NHS Trusts will include those that have contracts with independent healthcare providers that the Commission will regulate. The two bodies will, therefore, need to liaise and work together effectively. The intention of this provision is to help enable them to do so. All regulations made under this section must be made by the Secretary of State, but he may not make regulations enabling CHI's functions to be exercised by the Assembly without the agreement of the Assembly.

Section 10 Inquiries

56.   *Subsection (1)* enables the Secretary of State to act on any concerns over the Commission's exercise of its functions, by setting up an inquiry. *Subsection (2)* allows the Secretary of State to set up an inquiry into any matter connected with a regulated service. For example, if a consultant surgeon working in a private hospital was found to have unusually high death rates among his patients, the Secretary of State could set up an inquiry to investigate. *Subsections (3)* and *(4)* enable an inquiry to be held in private. This might be necessary to protect, for example, a victim of child abuse.

57.   *Subsection (5)* provides for section 250 (2) to (5) of the Local Government Act 1972 to apply in relation to an inquiry. This will enable the person holding the inquiry to issue a summons requiring an individual to give evidence or produce any documents in their custody or under their control at a stated time and place. If that person fails to attend (for reasons other than not having the necessary expenses of their visit paid or tendered), they are liable to a fine or imprisonment.

58.   *Subsection (6)* provides for the Assembly to have similar powers to those referred to in paragraph 56 above.

59.   *Subsection (7)* requires that reports of inquiries set up under the powers in this section should be published unless the appropriate Minister considers that there are exceptional circumstances that make publication inappropriate. Grounds for not publishing may include, for example, publication being prejudicial to ongoing criminal investigations or proceedings.

PART II ESTABLISHMENTS AND AGENCIES

60.   **Part II** makes provision for registration, the registration procedure, regulations and standards, offences and miscellaneous provision. Section*s 11* to *20* set out the provision for registration and the regulatory procedures to be followed by the registration authority. Provision for a right of appeal against decisions of the registration authority is made in *section 21*. *Section 22* provides regulation making powers for the appropriate Minister to make provision as respects management and staffing, fitness of premises and the conduct of any services regulated under Part II.   Section 22 will not apply to adoption agencies.   The regulations governing their procedures will continue to be made under the Adoption Act 1976, as amended by the Act to match the provisions of section 22. *Section 23* enables the appropriate Minister to issue national minimum standards for England or Wales applicable to all regulated services.   Any breach of these standards will not, of itself, be a breach of regulatory requirements, but the standards shall be taken into account when determining whether a breach of the regulations has occurred. *Sections 24* to *30* provide for offences under this Part, and *sections 31* to *42* make miscellaneous and supplemental provision.

Registration

61.   *Sections 11* to *20* set out the procedures which underpin the registration process, the registration authorities' day-to-day activities of considering applications for registration, conditions of registration, cancellation of registration and procedures for notifying applicants or providers of decisions. *Section 21* provides for rights of appeal.   The establishments and agencies in respect of which registration is required are those defined in *sections 1* to *4*.

Section 10 Requirement to register
62.   *Subsection (1)* provides that any person who carries on or manages an establishment or agency of any description must be registered, and it will be an offence to carry on or manage such an establishment without being registered in respect of it. The principle is that each establishment or agency should have a registered owner or proprietor (person who 'carries on' the business). If the person who carries on the business is not in day-to-day control of it, it is intended that the regulations will require the appointment of a manager who must also be registered by the registration authority (see *section 22*). *Subsection (2)* provides that an agency operating from several branches must register each branch separately.

63.   *Subsection (3)* – registration is required in respect of voluntary adoption agencies under the provisions of Part II, but the relevant sanctions remain within section 11 of the Adoption Act 1976.

64.   *Subsection (4)* enables the Secretary of State to make provision about registers to be kept by the Commission.

65.   *Subsections (5) and (6)* relate to offences. A person who carries on or manages an establishment or agency without being registered will be guilty of an offence and liable to a fine up to level 5 on the *standard scale**. If the person continues to run an unregistered establishment or agency after having been convicted of this offence, or after their registration has been cancelled, then they will be guilty of an offence and liable to six months' imprisonment, or a fine, or both.

Section 12 Applications for registration

66.   This section sets out the framework for applications for registration, with *subsection (1)* requiring that the application for registration must be made to the registration authority. *Subsection (3)* requires that a person applying for registration as a manager of an establishment or agency must be an individual, and not other types of legal 'person', such as a limited company or local authority. (See also the notes to *sections 22* and *56*, which together provide that a manager may be required to register on an appropriate part of the Council's register of social care workers.)

Section 13 Grant or refusal of registration

67.   Registration will only be granted if the registration authority is satisfied that the applicant has demonstrated that they have complied or will comply with all relevant requirements. The burden of proof is with the applicant rather than the registration authority.

68.   *Subsection (2)* provides that if the registration authority is satisfied that the applicant is complying or will comply with any requirements set out in regulations under *section 22* and the requirements of any other legislation which appears to the registration authority to be relevant, it must grant the application for registration, otherwise it must refuse it. If it grants the application, it must issue a certificate of registration *(subsection (4))*.

69.   *Subsection (3)* provides that the registration authority will be able to grant an application either unconditionally or subject to such conditions as it thinks fit. Conditions may be generic or specific. For example, the registration authority will be able to impose conditions on care homes specifying the categories of patients and the number of residents that may be accommodated. In some cases a specific condition may be required to take account of the circumstances in that individual home, centre, agency, private hospital or clinic. For example, there might be a condition that a particular door be kept locked to prevent confused residents from wandering directly on to a busy road.

---

* See paragraph 97 of these notes for definition of standard scale.

70.   *Subsection (5)* The registration authority may vary or remove a condition of registration at any time or impose an additional condition.

Section 14 Cancellation of registration
71.   This section gives the registration authority the power to cancel the registration of a person in respect of an establishment or agency, where a condition of registration has been breached, where a regulatory requirement has been breached or where a relevant offence has been committed. Further grounds for cancelling registration may be specified in regulations. Registration can be formally cancelled, even if an owner closes the establishment or agency before the cancellation process has been completed. This will ensure that the owner's record accurately reflects the situation, and they will not be able to open a new home elsewhere without the registration authority being aware of the previous history.

72.   Relevant offences for the purposes of section 14 are -

- failure to comply with conditions (*section 24*);
- contravention of regulations (*section 25*);
- false description of an establishment or agency (*section 26*);
- false statements in applications (*section 27*)
- failure to display a certificate of registration (*section 28*);
- obstructing an inspector (*section 31*);
- the offence of contravening regulations under section 9(2) of the Adoption Act 1976;
- any offence under the Children Act 1989 or any regulations made under it;
- offences under regulations made under section 1(3) of the Adoption (Intercountry Aspects) Act 1999;
- offences under the Registered Homes Act 1984 or regulations made under it.

73.   Cancellation of registration would not normally be the first step in a formal enforcement action. It is more likely to be used where other actions such as prosecution have failed to ensure compliance by the establishment or agency. If a registered person is convicted of a relevant offence, such as breaching a condition of registration (an offence under *section 24*), and still fails to remedy the breach, the registration authority will be able to consider cancellation of the person's registration.

Section 15 Applications by registered persons
74.   *Subsection (1)* enables the registered person to apply for a change to their conditions of registration (for example to change the number of people accommodated in the home) or to apply voluntarily for the cancellation of registration, for example, if they plan to close or sell

the business. *Subsection (2)* prevents a person voluntarily cancelling his registration if the registration authority have given notice of intention to, or decided to, cancel registration. *Subsection (3)* enables the appropriate Minister to make regulations specifying the particulars to accompany such an application, including provision for a prescribed fee. *Subsection (4)* provides that if the registration authority grant the application they must give notice in writing and issue a new certificate of registration.

Section 16 Regulations about registration

75.   *Section 16* provides for regulation-making powers with respect to registration. Regulations covering applications for registration *(subsection (1)(a))* will deal with matters such as the information that should be provided in the application. Regulations made under *subsection (1)(b)* may require certificates of registration to include, for example, the conditions of registration for that person in respect of that establishment or agency *eg* the categories of person a care home may accommodate.

76.   *Subsection (2)* concerns fostering and adoption agencies. The appropriate Minister will be able to make regulations to provide that fostering agencies or voluntary adoption agencies which are unincorporated bodies are ineligible to apply to be registered. This provision restates section 9(1) of the Adoption Act in respect of voluntary adoption societies (which is to be repealed) and applies it to fostering agencies.

77.   *Subsection (3)* enables regulations to be made requiring registered persons to pay an annual fee. These may be set at different levels or on a different basis for different types of organisation. Decisions will be made about the level and structuring of fees at a later date. *Subsection (4)* provides that unpaid fees may be recovered in the Magistrate's court.

Registration procedure

Sections 17 to 19 Notices and right to make representations

78.   *Section 17* provides for the registration authority to give notice of decisions it intends to take ("notice of proposal") with respect to applications for registration, cancellation of registration or any change to the conditions of registration. Notice must be given to the applicant or registered person and must set out the reasons *(subsection (6))*. For example, in the case of a person applying for registration for the first time, the notice of proposal will state whether or not the registration authority proposes to register them, and if so, the conditions subject to which they propose to grant the application. Section 17 does not apply where the registration authority decides to grant an application for registration unconditionally, or subject to agreed conditions.

79.   *Section 18* states that a notice given under section 17 must indicate that the person can, if they so wish, make written representations to the registration authority within a time limit of 28 days *(subsection (1))*. This stage ensures that the applicant has the opportunity to make their point of view known. *Subsection (2)* provides that the registration authority may not

make a decision until the 28 day period has ended unless they receive representations during the 28 day period or the person notifies the registration authority that he will not be making representations.

80.　　Once the representations stage has been completed, *section 19* requires the registration authority to serve a notice in writing of their decision on the applicant. The notice must explain the right of appeal conferred by *section 21* and in the case of a decision to grant an application subject to conditions or to vary conditions, set out those conditions. A decision to cancel registration, to grant an application subject to conditions which are not agreed, or to or change conditions will take effect only after the outcome of any appeal has been determined, or after 28 days if no appeal is brought. In the case of a decision to grant an application subject to conditions which are not agreed, if the applicant decides not to pursue his appeal the decision will take effect immediately.

Section 20 Urgent procedure for cancellation etc.

81.　　This section provides that the registration authority may apply to a justice of the peace for the immediate cancellation of registration or change in the conditions of registration of an establishment or agency. The justice may only make the order where it appears to him that unless the order is made there is a serious risk to a person's life, health or well-being. An order made under this section has immediate effect. It is intended to provide for a fast track procedure for appeals to the Tribunal against orders made under this section (see *section 21*).

82.　　*Subsection (3)* requires the registration authority to notify the local authority and Health Authority as well as any other statutory authority it considers appropriate, of the making of an urgent application. This is necessary so that the local authority can comply with their statutory duties as required, for example to provide or arrange alternative care for the service users in accordance with their duties under section 47(1) of the National Health Service and Community Care Act 1990, and that the Health Authority may consider whether to make provision for NHS services. It will be important that all statutory bodies that may be affected by the cancellation of a provider's registration have as much notice as possible to make any necessary arrangements. *Subsection (7)* defines a statutory authority for this purpose.

Section 21 Appeals to the Tribunal

83.　　*Section 21* provides for an appeal against a decision of the registration authority under Part II. The appeal is to the Tribunal established under section 9 of the Protection of Children Act 1999. *Subsections (3)* to *(5)* provide for the Tribunal's powers on considering an appeal.

Regulations and standards

84.　　*Section 22* provides regulation-making powers which will cover the management, staff, premises and conduct of establishments and agencies (other than voluntary adoption agencies). It also provides for regulations to be made regarding the welfare of service users.

Section 23 gives the appropriate Minister the power to publish statements of national minimum standards with which establishments and agencies are expected to comply. They are to be taken into account as stated in *subsection (4)*. For example, a regulation made under section 22 might state that suitable and nutritious food should be provided to all residents in a home. The national minimum standards would set out what registered providers are expected to provide in terms of the number of meals per day and their nutritional content.

85.   Different services will have different sets of regulations and standards which will be appropriate to the type of service.

Section 22 Regulation of establishments or agencies

86.   *Subsection (1)* provides a general power to make regulations imposing any requirements as the appropriate Minister thinks fit. *Subsection (2)* amplifies this, providing for regulations to be made that will be key to the registration of establishments and agencies. It will be essential that the registration authority can ensure establishments and agencies are carried on or managed by persons who are fit to do so. This subsection allows regulations to be made to ensure that establishments and agencies are suitably managed, staffed and equipped and that premises are fit for their purpose.

87.   *Subsection (2) (d)* provides powers to make regulations regarding the welfare of persons accommodated in establishments or provided with services by them, or who use the services of an independent medical agency or domiciliary care agency. *Subsection (2) (e)* provides similar powers to make regulations to secure the welfare of children placed by independent fostering agencies.

88.   *Subsections (3) and (4)* provide that regulations may be made prohibiting a person's appointment as manager of, or employment in, an establishment or agency unless they are on a register of social care workers, maintained under *section 56*.

89.   *Subsections (5)* and *(6)* provide that the welfare regulation making powers in 22 (2) (d) and (e) may cover the protection and promotion of health, the control and restraint of adults, and the control and restraint and discipline of children. This will enable regulations to set out what is acceptable behaviour management for adults and children.

90.   *Subsection (7)* gives the appropriate Minister power to make provision as to the conduct of an establishment or agency, including the provision of facilities and services, record keeping, notification of events, arrangements for dealing with complaints and in relation to independent hospitals and clinics, the arrangements to be made to secure that any medical or psychiatric treatment or listed services meet appropriate standards.

91.   *Subsections (7)(h)* and *(i)*. Just as it will be important for the registration authority to be made aware of a change in the person managing a home or branch of an agency, so will it be important to have notice of changes in the ownership or the officers of a company which

was registered in respect of a service. Fit person checks of company officers have a cost, and so in order to satisfy itself that the officers of the company taking over are fit persons, the registration authority would need to carry out these checks and be able to charge for this.

92.   *Subsection (8)* concerns regulations made in respect of secure accommodation for children, which may cover both its provision and its use, and facilities for religious instruction in children's homes.

93.   *Subsection (9)* requires the appropriate Minister to consult such persons as he considers appropriate before making or significantly amending regulations under the powers in this section.

94.   *Subsection (10)* Voluntary adoption agencies are excepted from the regulation-making powers set out in this section as equivalent provision is being made for them through amendments to the Adoption Act 1976 (see *Schedule 4, paragraph 5(6)(b)*).

Section 23 National minimum standards

95.   *Section 23* provides for the appropriate Minister to prepare and publish national minimum standards applicable to establishments and agencies. These will specify the standards applicable to the services and which, as *subsection (4)* makes clear, must be taken into account by a registration authority when making any decision, or in any proceedings for an offence under regulations under Part II. The standards may include parts of the GSCC codes of conduct and practice for employers of social care staff (see note to *section 62*).

Offences

96.   *Sections 24* to *30* set out the offences under this Part of the Act. The registration authority will be the prosecuting authority in respect of these offences, using the powers of entry and inspection under *section 31* and *section 32* to gather evidence.

97.   The registration authority will have two possible routes for enforcement action where a provider is not fulfilling their obligations: they can prosecute, or they can take action that may ultimately lead to cancellation of registration (see sections 14 and 20). It is intended that both courses of action could be pursued at the same time, if necessary. If convicted of an offence under this Part the registered person would be liable to the prescribed fine, as per the *standard scale*[*], or in some cases, imprisonment. Similar provisions for offences, including

---

[*] There are five levels to the *standard scale* for fines as defined in section 75 of the Criminal Justice Act 1982. A court may impose a fine up to the maximum for the prescribed level. Currently the levels are: level 1 = £200; level 2 = £500; level 3 = £1,000; level 4 = £2,500 and level 5 = £5,000.

those with regard to proceedings and offences by bodies corporate, were made under the Registered Homes Act 1984 in Part IV (sections 46 to 53).

Section 24 Failure to comply with conditions

98.   Where the conditions of registration are not adhered to without reasonable excuse, the registration authority may prosecute.

Section 25 Contravention of regulations

99.   *Subsection (1)* provides that regulations made under this Part may provide that a failure to comply with the regulations will be an offence. It is intended that the regulations will provide that the registration authority may serve a notice in respect of a breach of a regulatory requirement, requiring it to be remedied within a specified period. If at the end of that period the breach has not been remedied, the person shall be guilty of an offence. *Subsection (2)* provides the fine shall not exceed level 4 on the standard scale.

Section 26 False descriptions of establishments and agencies.

100.   *Section 26* makes it an offence for a person to describe any premises as a particular kind of establishment or agency when it is not registered as such. This would catch, for example, an unscrupulous hotel proprietor who tried to pretend his hotel was a nursing home. It would also catch registered persons who misrepresent the nature of their establishment, by claiming it is suitable for a particular category of resident when it is not. The penalty on summary conviction is a fine not exceeding level 5 on the standard scale.

Section 27 False statements in applications

101.   This section makes it an offence for an applicant knowingly to make a false or misleading statement in applications to the registration authority. The penalty will be a fine of up to level 4 on the standard scale. The application forms will inform people of this offence, which should act as a strong incentive for people to complete their applications accurately.

Section 28 Failure to display certification of registration

102.   *Section 28* makes it an offence not to display a certificate of registration. The penalty on summary conviction is a fine not exceeding level 2 on the standard scale.

Section 29 Proceedings for offences

103.   *Section 29* provides that proceedings in respect of offences under Part II may not be taken by any person, without the consent of the Attorney General, other than the Commission or, in the context of his default powers the Secretary of State; or the National Assembly for Wales. *Subsection (2)* extends the time allowed for proceedings to be brought in respect of offences under this Part. The usual limit for the prosecution of summary offences is six months after the offence is committed. However, in some cases, offences may only come to light after an inspection or whistleblowing. Subsection (2) therefore provides for a six month time limit from when the offence comes to light, with an overall time limit of three years from the commission of the offence.

Section 30 Offences by bodies corporate

104.   *Subsection (2)* provides that if an offence under Part II is proved to have been committed with the consent or connivance of an officer of a body corporate then he as well as the company are guilty of the offence.   Individual officers of a body corporate who are complicit in an offence under this Part of the Act, will not be able to escape prosecution simply because the body corporate is liable: both may be liable to prosecution.

Miscellaneous and Supplemental

Section 31 Inspections by persons authorised by the registration authority

105.   *Subsection (1)* provides that the registration authority may require a person who carries on or manages an establishment or agency to provide it with any information to enable the registration authority to discharge its functions.   *Subsection (2)* enables a person authorised by the registration authority to enter and inspect premises at any time if they are used or he believes them to be used as an establishment or for the purposes of an agency. These powers are necessary to ensure compliance with the regulatory framework.

106.   Inspectors may also require relevant records or other documents to be produced for inspection on the premises wherever they may be kept, and where they are stored on computer, that they are produced in a legible, not encrypted, form.   Inspectors will also be able to copy or remove relevant records (other than medical records), and will be able to interview, in private, the manager, employees, or any patients or persons accommodated or cared for there who consent to be interviewed *(subsections (3) and (4))*.

107.   *Subsections (5) and (6)* allow a medical practitioner or registered nurse to examine in private, with their consent, a patient or resident, or their medical records, where they believe that the person may not be receiving proper care.   If the person is incapable of giving their consent, a medical practitioner or registered nurse may still examine them and/ or their medical records if they believe they have not been receiving proper care.

108.   *Subsection (7)* provides for a regulation-making power to determine the minimum frequency of inspections of premises by a registration authority, and *subsection (8)* requires inspectors to produce appropriate documentation showing their right to enter and inspect the premises if required so to do.

109.   *Subsection (9)* makes it an offence for a person to intentionally obstruct the exercise of the powers under this section or *section 32*.   The penalty on summary conviction is a fine not exceeding level 4 on the standard scale.

Section 32 Inspections: supplementary

110.   *Section 32* allows a person (authorised to enter and inspect premises by virtue of section 31) to remove any material *etc.* which could be used as evidence of possible non-

compliance with requirements. *Subsection (2)* imposes a requirement to assist the authorised person and permits the authorised person to take such measurements and photographs and make such recordings as he considers necessary to enable him to exercise his powers under this section. *Subsection (5)* requires the registration authority to prepare a report after carrying out an inspection under section 31 and send a copy of the report to the registered persons. *Subsection (6)* provides that the registration authority must make the report available to the public. *Subsection (8)* provides that in England, inspection reports shall be made available in the regional offices of the Commission in the region in which the premises are situated.

Section 33 Annual Returns

111.   *Section 33* enables the appropriate Minister to make regulations requiring the person carrying on an establishment or agency to provide the registration authority with an annual return to include whatever details and cover whatever period of time is prescribed.

Section 34 Liquidators etc.

112.   *Section 34* enables the appropriate Minister to make regulations such that if an establishment or agency were to go into receivership or liquidation, the liquidator must inform the registration authority of his appointment. The regulations will require the liquidator to appoint a suitably qualified manager.

Section 35 Death of registered person

113.   *Subsection (1)* enables the appropriate Minister to make provision in regulations for what is to happen in a case where a person who was the only person registered in respect an establishment or agency dies. This might be the case if a person carrying on a care home is also in control of its day to day running. The personal representatives will be required to notify the registration authority. *Subsection (2)* enables the regulations to specify the period during which the personal representatives will be allowed to carry on the business. The regulations will permit the registration authority to decide whether it is appropriate for a personal representative or relative to carry on running the establishment or agency for a further period.

Section 36 Provision of copies of registers

114.   *Subsection (1)* provides that copies of any register which it has to keep are available for inspection. A person may be provided with a copy or extracts of a register on request (*subsection (2)*). A charge may be made except where prescribed in regulations or the registration authority decides it should be provided free. However, it would not be acceptable to release some information contained in registers, for example a list of children's homes in a given area.   *Subsection (3)* therefore enables regulations to be made providing that the register may not be inspected, or copies of the register or extracts are not to be made available, in such circumstances as the appropriate Minister may prescribe.

Section 37 Service of documents

115.   *Section 37* makes provisions about service of documents. They may be delivered personally or sent by registered letter or recorded delivery. Service will be deemed to have taken place on the third day after the day on which the document is sent.

Section 38 Transfers of staff under Part II

116.   *Section 38* makes provision for the appropriate Minister to transfer eligible staff from Health Authority and local authority inspection units to the registration authority. Their existing contract of employment will have effect as if made between the designated members of staff and the registration authority (see notes to *sections 114* and *115*).

Section 39 Temporary extension of meaning of "nursing home"

117.   *Section 39* makes interim provision for the regulation of dental practitioners using premises for the wholly private treatment of patients under general anaesthesia. Responsibility for the registration of such premises will ultimately pass from the Health Authority to the Commission or the Assembly. The section amends the existing exemptions under the Registered Homes Act 1984, which had previously excepted all premises used by dental practitioners for the treatment of their patients, unless the treatment involved the use of class 3B and 4 lasers. This provision will have effect for the period during which the Registered Homes Act remains in force.

Section 40 Temporary extension of meaning of "children's home"

118.   *Section 40* makes interim provision for the regulation of small private children's homes accommodating fewer than four children. This section amends the definition of "children's home" in section 63 of the Children Act 1989 so as to require small children's homes to be registered. This will have the effect of requiring these homes to be registered with local authorities under existing legislation until such time as the registration provisions in Part II are commenced, at which point the responsibility will pass to the Commission or the Assembly.

Section 41 Children's homes temporary provision about cancellation of registration

119.   This section makes provision about the cancellation of registration of all children's homes, for to cover the period up to full implementation of Part II of the Act. In particular, it will apply to small homes required to register under the Children Act for the first time by section 40. Registration can be formally cancelled, even if an owner closes the establishment or agency before the cancellation process has been completed. This will ensure that the owner's record accurately reflects the situation, and they will not be able to open a new home elsewhere without the registration authority being aware of past history.

Section 42 Power to extend application of Part II

120.   This section makes provision, through regulations, for the future registration of other services which are not covered on the face of the Act. The services concerned are those that are, or are similar to services which local authorities provide in the exercise of their social services functions, or similar to those provided by certain NHS bodies. An example of such a

local authority service would be day care for adults. NHS-type services to which this provision may apply include, for example, treatment provided in private patients' own homes through future developments in telecare and telemedicine. The extension could also be applied to agencies that supply staff who provide any of these services.

PART III LOCAL AUTHORITY SERVICES

121.   **Part III** concerns local authority fostering and adoption services. The principle behind these provisions is that all such services, whoever provides them, should be required to meet the same standards. The registration authority will inspect these services, using powers in *sections 45* and *46*, applying equivalent standards as for voluntary adoption agencies and independent fostering agencies registered under Part II. Local authority provision will not be registered, but where an authority is found to be failing in England the National Care Standards Commission must report the authority to the Secretary of State. In Wales, the registration authority will report the matter to the relevant part of the National Assembly for Wales, which will take appropriate action.

Section 43 Introductory
122.   This section defines the functions that are subject to inspection by the registration authority. In respect of adoption, the relevant functions are those of making or participating in arrangements for the adoption of children. These are the local authority functions with respect to which regulations may be made by virtue of section 9(3) of the Adoption Act 1976, and which are also carried out by voluntary adoption agencies (which will be regulated under Part II of this Act). The relevant functions cover, in particular, the approval of prospective adopters, the preparation of children for adoption and the making of adoptive placements.

123.   In respect of fostering, the relevant functions are those which are capable of being delegated to other bodies by virtue of regulations made under paragraph 12(g) of Schedule 2 to the Children Act 1989. They include the approval of foster parents, the placement of children on behalf of the local authority, and the supervision of the placement. Bodies which act for local authorities under delegated powers are to be regulated as fostering agencies under Part II of this Act. Relevant functions for these purposes do not extend to any of the local authority's discretionary duties in respect of children it is looking after, for example to safeguard and promote welfare, to decide on the type of placement and to review their cases. Such duties may not be delegated.

Section 44 General powers of the Commission
124.   *Section 44*, which provides that the Commission may give advice to the Secretary of State in respect of Part III matters, mirrors the provision in respect of Part II services in section 7(5). The Commission may therefore advise the Secretary of State of any changes

that need to be made to secure improvements in the quality of local authority fostering and adoption services, and of any changes that may need to be made to the national minimum standards provided for in *section 49*.

Sections 45 and 46 Inspection of relevant adoption and fostering services

125. These sections provide for the inspection of relevant adoption and fostering services. To a large extent these provisions mirror those in sections 31 and 32, which provide for similar powers to be exercised in relation to the regulation of independent fostering agencies and voluntary adoption agencies. The powers in these two sections are wide and are exercisable by a person so authorised by the registration authority.

Section 45 Inspection by registration authority of adoption and fostering services

126. *Section 45* relates closely to section 31. *Subsection (1)(a)* obliges an authority to provide whatever information the authorised person requires and *subsection (1)(b)* provides for the entry and inspection of premises used by the authority in the discharge of relevant adoption and foster care functions. *Subsections (2)* and *(3)* make provision about access to documents and records, including computer records, and provides for an authorised person to interview in private any employee of the authority. If records are stored on a computer they must be produced in a legible, not encrypted, form. *Subsection (4)* provides for a regulation making power to determine the frequency of inspections.

127. *Subsection (5)* applies section 31(8) and (9), which provide for the proper identification of a person exercising powers of entry and inspection on behalf of the registration authority, and for offences. Obstruction or a failure to comply with inspection requirements without reasonable excuse is a summary offence, punishable by a fine at level 4 on the standard scale.

Section 46 Inspections: supplementary

128. *Section 46* relates closely to section 32. *Subsection (1)* permits an authorised person to remove any document or other material on the premises as evidence of possible non-compliance with the regulatory requirements (as defined by *subsection (7)*). *Subsection (2)* imposes a requirement to assist the authorised person, and permits the authorised person to take measurements and photographs and make recordings, for example, a tape or video recording, in the exercise of his inspection powers. *Subsection (3)* provides the authorised person with a right of access to computers.

129. *Subsection (4)* requires the registration authority to prepare a report after carrying out an inspection under this Part, and to send a copy of this report to the local authority as soon as possible. *Subsections (5)* and *(6)* provide that the registration authority must make the report available to the public.

130. *Subsection (7)* identifies the regulatory requirements that apply to this section and section 45. These are:

- requirements set out in regulations made under *section 48*;

- regulations made under section 23(2)(a) of the Children Act 1989 (at present, the Foster Placement (Children) Regulations 1991 (SI 1991 No 910) (as amended) and Arrangements for Placement of Children (General) Regulations 1991 (SI 1991 No 890) (as amended);

- regulations made under section 9(3) of the Adoption Act (at present, the Adoption Agencies Regulations 1983 (SI 1983 No 1964) (as amended);

- regulations made under the Adoption (Intercountry Aspects) Act 1999 (none yet in force).

131.   *Subsection (8)* provides that, in England, inspection reports shall be made available in the regional offices of the Commission in the region in which the relevant local authority is situated.

Section 47 Action following inspection
132.   This section deals with the action to be taken by the Commission following inspection of a local authority in England. By *subsection (1)* the Commission must notify the Secretary of State at any time if it considers that a local authority does not satisfy the regulatory requirements, where the failure is substantial.

133.   The Commission must also report to the Secretary of State following the exercise of its powers of inspection, and at the expiry of any time limit for improvement specified in a notice given to the local authority under *subsection (5)* (see below). At such times, the Secretary of State must be notified whether a local authority satisfies the regulatory requirements, or fails to do so.   Alternatively, the Commission may, if it considers appropriate, give the local authority a notice under *subsection (5)* and inform the Secretary of State that it has done so. A notice under subsection (5) specifies those areas or issues in which the authority fails to satisfy the regulatory requirements and what action it should take to remedy the failure.   The notice also imposes time constraints within which a failure should be remedied. At the end of the period specified in any notice, the Commission must notify the Secretary of State whether or not the local authority now satisfies the regulatory requirements.

134.   Where the Commission has made a report to the Secretary of State to the effect that a local authority is not meeting regulatory requirements, *subsection (6)* applies so that the Commission is relieved of its duty of inspection until the Secretary of State notifies the Commission that subsection (6) ceases to apply. The purpose of this provision is to avoid duplication of powers and duties in the event that the Secretary of State decides to take enforcement action in respect of the local authority.

135. These powers do not apply in Wales since the National Assembly for Wales will both undertake regulatory responsibility and have enforcement powers in respect of the local authority.

Section 48 Regulation of the exercise of relevant fostering functions
136. This section provides for regulations imposing requirements concerning the exercise of a local authority's relevant fostering functions as defined by section 43(3)(b). Parallel provision is made in respect of "relevant adoption functions" by amendment to section 9(3) of the Adoption Act 1976. The powers mirror, with necessary adjustments, those in section 22 with the intention that similar standards should apply to both local authority and independent sector services. Regulations may provide for the fitness of workers, the suitability of premises; management and control of operations; numbers and types of workers and their management and training. By *section 52* the regulations may provide that breach of a specified provision is a summary offence, punishable by a fine not exceeding level 4[*]. The equivalent power in the Adoption Act 1976 is in section 9(4), as amended by this Act.

Section 49 National minimum standards
137. This section empowers the appropriate Minister to prepare and publish national minimum standards applicable to relevant local authority adoption and fostering functions, mirroring the provision in Part II for voluntary adoption agencies and fostering agencies. As provided for in Part II, any new standards or significant changes must be subject to consultation before being issued, and a failure to comply with the national minimum standards will be taken into account by the registration authority in deciding whether a local authority has met the regulatory requirements.

Section 50 Annual Returns
138. This section, which mirrors section 33, makes provision about annual returns of information to be made by the local authority in respect of its relevant adoption and fostering functions.

Section 51 Annual fee
139. Regulations may be made requiring an annual fee of a prescribed amount to be payable to the registration authority by the local authority. Unpaid fees may be recovered in the Magistrate's court.

Section 52 Contravention of regulations
140. In parallel with Part II, regulations made under this Part may create offences.

---

[*] See paragraph 97 of these notes for definition of standard scale

Section 53 Offences: general provisions
141.   This section applies sections 29 (proceedings for offences) and 30 (offences by bodies corporate) to this Part.

PART IV: SOCIAL CARE WORKERS

142.   **Part IV** concerns the functions and procedures of the General Social Care Council (GSCC) and Care Council for Wales (CCW) (Cyngor Gofal Cymru), referred to collectively as "the Councils". Section*s 54 and 55* set out the definitions relevant to this Part of the Act. The Councils will maintain registers of social care workers, and the procedures for this are set out in *sections 56 to 60. Section 61* enables the title of "social worker" to be protected, by making it an offence to describe oneself as a social worker with intent to deceive, if not registered as a social worker with one of the Councils. *Section 62* concerns the Councils' responsibilities to develop and promulgate codes of practice for social care work. *Sections 63 to 66* set out the Councils' functions with regard to regulating the education and training of social workers, including requirements in respect of applicants with qualifications gained outside England and Wales.

143.   The Councils will both be established as non-departmental public bodies, with the GSCC being sponsored by the Department of Health, and the CCW being sponsored by the National Assembly for Wales. The Councils will operate according to rules, which they will draw up and which will need the approval of the Secretary of State for the GSCC in England, and the National Assembly for Wales for the CCW in Wales. Individuals will have a right of appeal to an independent Tribunal against the Councils' decisions not to register them or to remove them from the register.

144.   In the remainder of these notes, a reference to "the Council" means, in relation to England, the GSCC, and in relation to Wales, the CCW.

Preliminary

Section 54 and Schedule 1: Care Councils
145.   *Section 54* establishes the GSCC for England and the CCW for Wales.   The constitution of the Councils is set out in *Schedule 1*, which as indicated in paragraph 43 of these notes is a combined schedule setting out the arrangements for the National Care Standards Commission in England in addition to both of the Councils. The following points in Schedule 1 are of particular note with respect to the Councils:

146. *Paragraph 3: General powers.* This paragraph gives the Councils general powers, which may be subject to direction by the appropriate Minister. These include an express power for the Councils to co-operate with other public authorities in the United Kingdom. If the Councils are to undertake their functions properly and protect the public the English and Welsh Councils must be able to co-operate with each other, and also with equivalent bodies that might be established in Scotland and Northern Ireland. The sort of area in which the Councils would be expected to co-operate would be in exchanging information about people who had been refused registration, removed from a register or allowed qualified registration. Co-operation will be especially important where a person dealt with by one Council moves to another part of the UK. The power to co-operate with other public authorities will also give the Councils scope to co-operate with public regulatory bodies on other fields, such as the United Kingdom Central Council for Nursing, Midwifery and Health Visiting (the UKCC), where this can further the performance of their functions.

147. *Paragraph 5: Membership* The appropriate Minister will appoint the Chairman and members of each Council. In England, for example, it is intended that the GSCC will be only as big as is needed to secure the cost-effective discharge of its business, and is unlikely to exceed 25 people. The intention is that the Council will be composed of people representing all the key interests. Members will be appointed so that service users and lay members will be the majority of the Council. Appointments will be made after consultation with service user interests and by inviting applications from members of the public.

148. *Paragraph 7: Remuneration and allowances.* Remuneration and allowances for each Council will be matters for the appropriate Minister. For the GSCC, for example, it is intended to remunerate the chairman only. All members will be entitled to travel expenses and other costs associated with membership of the Council. It is not intended to make provision for pensions for the chairman or members of the Council.

149. *Paragraph 8: Chief officer.* The appropriate Minister will appoint the first chief officer of each of the Councils as this post will be filled ahead of the organisations being fully established to allow the first chief officers to assist their Chairmen with preparatory work including appointments of key staff. The Councils will appoint future chief officers themselves.

150. *Paragraph 13: Delegation of functions.* This gives the Council flexibility to discharge its business in the most efficient way, through the Council itself, its staff or others brought in for the purpose. Examples of outside assistance the Council might use are contracting with suitable outside bodies, using consultants or temporary staff on fixed term contracts depending on the work to be done. *Paragraph 14 (Arrangements for the use of staff)*, enables the Council to make arrangements with other bodies for use of their staff and *vice versa.*

151. *Paragraph 16: Payments to authorities.* The appropriate Minister can fund each Council from public money. Both Councils will be funded wholly through this route initially,

although in time it is intended that once the registers of social care staff are established fees from registration will contribute to the cost of the registration function, taking into account a suitable registration fee to charge a generally low paid workforce.

Section 55 Interpretation

152.   This section introduces terms used in this part of the Act. It provides a definition of "social care worker" for the purposes of the Councils, and allows for regulations to be made to include certain other classes of persons in this description. Social care worker is used as a generic term encompassing the majority of people who are employed in social care work.

153.   The section also defines "relevant social work", introduces the term social worker and provides a definition of a day centre. (See also notes on Part II – Registration).

Registration

Section 56 The register

154.   This section provides for the Council to establish and maintain a register of social care workers. There is to be a separate part of the register for social workers and for any other description of social care workers specified by the appropriate Minister by order. Applicants for registration must satisfy the requirements of *section 58*, including any training requirements imposed by the Council.

155.   The social care workforce is large, diverse and mainly unqualified. This sector has approximately one million staff in England and Wales, 80% of whom hold no relevant qualifications. With these low levels of qualifications in the workforce it is envisaged that registration will be incremental, by occupational group. Professional social workers, virtually all of whom are qualified, will be the first group of staff to be registered. In England the Government is funding the training of residential child care workers, as a priority group, to National Vocational Qualification (NVQ) level 3 to ensure that they are among the early registrants with the GSCC.

Sections 57 Applications for registration

156.   *Section 57* provides for the Council to make rules governing how applications to its register shall be made. The appropriate Minister will have to approve all rules made by the Council (see *section 71(2)*.

Section 58 Grant or refusal of registration

157.   *Section 58* lists the conditions an applicant must satisfy in order to be registered with the Council. Applicants must satisfy any requirements imposed by the Council as to training, conduct and competence. The Councils must also be satisfied as to an applicant's good character and that he is physically and mentally fit to perform the whole or part of the work of

persons registered in the part of the register to which his application refers. The Council must refuse an application for registration if it is not satisfied an applicant meets the conditions.

Section 59 Removal *etc* from the register

158.   This section provides for the Council to make rules about the circumstances under which a person can be removed or suspended from any part of the register. The section also makes provision for the procedure to be followed and as to rules of evidence in proceedings, which may be in public, by which the matter can be determined.

Section 60 Rules about registration

159.   *Section 60* provides a power for the Council to make rules governing registration. It is intended that the rules will cover evidence to be produced in support of an application for registration, the length of the registration period and renewal.

Section 61 Use of title "social worker" *etc*

160.   *Section 61* provides for protection of the title "social worker" by the creation of an offence, punishable by a fine up to level 5 on the standard scale[*] for a person who is not registered as a social worker to use that title or hold himself out as a registered social worker with an intention to deceive. An individual will not be guilty of an offence if they are registered with an equivalent regulatory body in another part of the UK. Registration as a social worker with the Council will give a stamp of approval to an individual as a professional and can give access to vulnerable people. This provision will be brought into force when the appropriate Minister thinks the time is right for it to add to the protection of the public.

Codes of Practice

Section 62 Codes of Practice

161.   By *section 62* the Council is required to produce codes of good practice for social care workers and for employers of such staff. No such nationally agreed codes exist at present. It is intended that drawing up and promulgating these codes will be the first task for the Council. Social care is a fast developing field, therefore the codes will not be static. The Council will be obliged to keep them under review and amend them where it thinks necessary, consulting representatives of social care workers. The appropriate Minister may incorporate relevant parts of them into the national minimum standards described in section 23 that will apply to services registered with the registration authorities.

---

[*] See paragraph 97 of these notes for definition of standard scale

Training

Sections 63 Approval of courses *etc*

162.   The Council will take over the regulation of professional social work training and related post-qualifying training from the Central Council for Education and Training in Social Work (CCETSW). *Section 63* gives wide powers to the Council to make rules about the approval of courses with the intention of ensuring the consistency and quality of the education to be provided for social workers at pre- and post-qualifying levels.

163.   It is essential that all social care training is appropriately regulated if standards in social care work are to be improved.   This is part of the main intention behind the establishment of the Councils. CCETSW has the statutory duty to regulate professional social work training only.   The new Councils will have functions in respect of training for all social care work. When CCETSW, which is a UK body, ceases to exercise its functions in relation to England and Wales, the regulation of professional social work training in England will be transferred to the GSCC, and training in Wales will be transferred to the CCW as the most appropriate bodies.   Scotland and Northern Ireland will legislate separately to create new arrangements for CCETSW's functions.

164.   National Vocational Qualifications (NVQs), the qualifications for the non-professional social care staff, are already regulated by the Qualifications and Curriculum Authority.   It would not be sensible to remove social care NVQs from these overall arrangements for NVQs for separate regulation.   The Council's function in respect of this type of training will be to make completion of particular NVQ courses a requirement to registration.   An example in England may be the registration of residential childcare workers, which would be likely to require qualification at NVQ level 3, as discussed in the commentary on section 56 earlier in these notes.

Section 64 Qualifications gained outside a Council's area

165.   The Council will register professional social workers on the basis of their having successfully completed a period of approved training. The GSCC will approve training in England, and the CCW will approve training in Wales. *Section 64(1)* provides for the GSCC to recognise, for the purposes of registration, qualifications gained outside England as being the equivalent of those gained through GSCC approved training in this country. *Section 64(2)* makes an equivalent provision for the CCW.   As each of the UK countries will have its own regulatory body for social care, this section applies to qualifications gained in Scotland, Wales and Northern Ireland as well as those gained in other EEA States and in other parts of the world.

Section 65 Post registration training

166.   It is common in other professions for continued registration with a regulatory body to be linked to continuing professional education and development. Continuing education is no less needed in social care, where safe, legal practice depends on an individual's updated

knowledge of research advances and developments in best practice. *Section 65* therefore makes provision for the Council to be able to make rules requiring registered persons to undertake additional training. The Council will consult relevant persons before making or later varying these rules.

Section 66 Visitors for certain social work courses

167.   As part of its powers to approve and monitor the effectiveness of individual training courses in social work, the Council will need to be able to visit and report on the places delivering this training. *Section 66* gives the Council powers to be able to appoint and pay the visitors to undertake this work on its behalf and to visit the place offering the training. Provision is made in respect of visits to both higher education institutes, which deliver the academic element of the training, and social services agencies that provide the practice placements where students can develop their practical skills.

Section 67 Functions of the appropriate Minister

168.   *Section 67* gives certain functions to the appropriate Minister, who can delegate such functions to the relevant Council. In addition, the Secretary of State may authorise any person to exercise his functions, and will be able to choose an appropriate person to carry out the function efficiently and effectively. In Wales, the Assembly can similarly authorise any person to exercise its functions.

169.   *Subsection (1)* gives the appropriate Minister responsibility to ascertain the training needs of the social care workforce and the financial and other assistance required to promote such training. He is also given responsibility to encourage provision of assistance, and for the drawing up of occupational standards in social care. In England these powers are intended to be delegated to the *Training Organisation for Personal Social Services* (TOPSS)*-England*. In Wales, these functions will be delegated to TOPSS-Wales.

170.   *Subsections (2) and (3)* establish the promotion of social care training as a function of the appropriate Minister, which he can devolve to the relevant Council. Promotion of social work training is one of the functions currently undertaken by CCETSW. This section extends the function so that it encompasses the promotion of training for all social care not just for professional social workers. Promotion of training includes publicising training opportunities, attracting potential students to training and providing information for social care staff and

---

* *TOPSS* is the National Training Organisation (NTO) for the social care sector. NTOs are an initiative by the Department for Education and Employment to provide each sector of industry with an employment-led body that has national responsibilities for workforce and training issues. TOPSS was established with assistance from the Department of Health and was established as an independent employment-led organisation from 1 April 2000. Employment interests from all sectors of social care are already represented on it. TOPSS has produced a National Training Strategy for England, which was distributed widely in the social care field in November 1999 for comment. TOPSS-England is the England arm of this UK body. The Welsh arm will be incorporated into the Care Council for Wales.

recruits enquiring about training. It is intended that in England, this function will also be devolved to TOPSS as the most suitable body.

171.   *Subsection (4)* of this section gives the appropriate Minister the power to pay grants and allowances to students and grants to organisations involved in training. In England it is intended that the Secretary of State will devolve the power to pay these grants to the GSCC.

Miscellaneous and supplemental

Section 68: Appeals to the Tribunal
172.   This section gives individuals the right of appeal to an independent Tribunal, defined in *section 121(1)* as the Tribunal established under the Protection of Children Act 1999. Individuals will have a right of appeal against decisions by the Council, in respect of registration, (for example, a decision not to register them or to remove them from the register). Such decisions could affect an individual's ability to secure employment so access to an independent tribunal is essential.

Section 69: Publication etc of the register
173.   *Section 69* requires the Council to make its register publicly available. It is intended that the Council will make the register available on the Internet and will also publish it in hard copy annually.

Section 70 Abolition of CCETSW
174.   *Section 70* abolishes CCETSW in relation to England and Wales. It enables a scheme to be made under an Order in Council to make provision in consequence of CCETSW ceasing to exercise functions in relation to a part of the United Kingdom. The scheme may provide for the transfer of staff and for disposing of the assets and liabilities of CCETSW. Scotland and Northern Ireland will legislate separately to set up new arrangements for dealing with the functions of CCETSW in those countries.

Section 71 Rules
175.   This section refers to the power of the Council to make rules about the issues in Part IV of the Act, allowing the Council flexibility in how far any particular rule may extend. For example, rules may be made in relation to all cases to which a power to make rules extends, or in relation to cases that are specified in the rules. *Subsections (2)* and *(3)* concern rules about the charging of fees in connection with the Council's functions. For example, fees may be charged for registration, approval of courses, provision of training or providing codes of practice or copies of or extracts from the register. *Subsection (4)* provides that all rules made by the Council under this Part are subject to the approval of the appropriate Minister.

PART V – THE CHILDREN'S COMMISSIONER FOR WALES

176. Part V establishes an office of the Children's Commissioner for Wales, and sets out its functions and powers. These will extend to all the services for children regulated in Wales under the Act: children's homes, residential family centres, local authority fostering and adoption services, fostering agencies, voluntary adoption agencies, domiciliary care services for children, the welfare aspects of daycare and childminding services for all children under the age of eight; and the welfare of children living away from home in boarding schools. They will also apply to children in other settings regulated under this Act, such as care homes and independent hospitals. The Commissioner's functions and powers include the review and monitoring of arrangements for dealing with complaints, 'whistleblowing' and advocacy arrangements; the examination of particular cases; and providing assistance, including financial, to a child in making a complaint or in other proceedings.

Section 72 Children's Commissioner for Wales
177. *Section 72* establishes the office of the Children's Commissioner for Wales (or Comisiynydd Plant Cymru), and gives effect to *Schedule 2*. Schedule 2 sets out arrangements for the constitution, appointment, financial and audit procedures and other general provisions.

Section 73 Review and monitoring of arrangements
178. *Section 73* sets out what the Commissioner may do in respect of ensuring that arrangements for complaints, whistleblowing and advocacy procedures in respect of children's services regulated in Wales under this Act safeguard and promote the rights and welfare of children receiving such services.

179. *Subsections (2), (3) and (4)* give details of the arrangements that the Commissioner is empowered to monitor and review. *Subsection (2)* concerns complaints or representations made by, or on behalf of, children to whom this Part applies. *Subsection (3)* concerns the arrangements for ensuring proper action is taking following disclosure of information (*ie* whistleblowing). Such information may appear to show that a criminal offence has been committed, that a legal obligation has not been fulfilled, that the health and safety of a person has been endangered, or that any of these have been deliberately concealed. *Subsection (4)* concerns arrangements for advocacy or other support (as may be described in regulations) for children.

Section 74 Examination of cases
180. *Subsection (1)* enables the Assembly to make regulations giving the Commissioner power to examine the cases of particular relevant children to whom regulated services are provided. Under *subsection (2)* provision is made for regulations to detail the circumstances in which an examination may be made; the procedure for conducting an examination; and the publication of reports following examination. *Subsection (3)* enables the regulations to be made granting the Commissioner rights to obtain information, explanations and assistance in respect of such an examination. For the purposes of examination, *subsection (4)* provides that

the Commissioner shall have the same powers as the High Court in respect of the attendance and examination of witnesses and the production of documents.

Section 75 Obstruction *etc*

181.   This section give the Commissioner power to complain to the High Court if he is obstructed in the exercise of his powers, as set out above. The High Court can then deal with the person concerned as if they were obstructing the High Court in the exercise of its functions. This is a common form of enforcement mechanism for offices of this type.

Section 76 Further functions

182.   *Subsections (1)* and *(2)* enable the Assembly to make regulations giving the Commissioner power to assist a child (including financially) who is making a complaint or representation to, or in respect of, a provider; or who is taking part in any prescribed proceedings. *Subsection (3)* enables the Commissioner to give advice and information to any person in connection with his functions. *Subsection (4)* enables further functions to be conferred on the Commissioner in regulations, in connection with his existing functions under this Part. *Subsection (6)* sets out restrictions on naming persons who are not the subject of an investigation in reports of the Commissioner. *Subsection (7)* establishes that the publication of any matter by the Commissioner in a report arising from his functions is absolutely privileged for the purposes of the law of defamation.

Section 77 Restrictions

183.   *Subsection (1)* restricts the Commissioner's ability to enquire into or report on any matter that is or has been the subject of legal proceedings before a court or tribunal. *Subsection (2)* precludes the Commissioner from exercising any functions which under statute is exercisable by another individual or body, eg CAFCASS (the Children and Family Court Advisory Support Service), if regulations so provide.

Section 78 Interpretation

184.   This section provides definitions for this Part of the Act. *Subsection (1)* provides that this Part of the Act applies to a child in respect of whom regulated children's services are provided in Wales. For example, a child accommodated in a children's home, or in foster care. *Subsections (2)* to *(5)* define the term "regulated children's services in Wales", and provide further clarification as to who is to be treated as the provider of particular regulated services.

185.   *Subsection (6)* enables the Assembly to provide, in regulations, for the Commissioner to exercise his functions in respect of a matter that occurred prior to the commencement of this Part, and in respect of an adult who was a child receiving relevant services during a prescribed time. This will enable the Commissioner to investigate cases that come to light after his Office is established, even though the events took place prior to that time.

PART VI – CHILD MINDING AND DAY CARE FOR YOUNG CHILDREN

186.   **Part VI** inserts a new Part (Part XA) into the Children Act 1989 which provides for child minding and day care for young children in England and Wales. Part X of the Children Act continues to apply to Scotland. In England the responsibility for child minding and day care regulation is transferred from local authorities to Her Majesty's Chief Inspector of Schools for England (HMCIS). The functions will be brought together with those in respect of the inspection of nursery education under a new Early Years Directorate within Ofsted.

187.   In addition, the new Part XA makes changes to the present system of child minding and day care regulation. For example, it gives the Secretary of State powers to make regulations governing the activities of registered providers (such as in respect of qualifications and training or the safety of premises) and introduces a requirement to publish inspection reports. In Wales the responsibility for child minding and day care regulation will pass to the registration authority established as part of the National Assembly for Wales. Her Majesty's Chief Inspector of Education and Training in Wales, working through Estyn (the Welsh equivalent of Ofsted), will continue to inspect early years education under existing powers.

188.   In addition, the new Part XA provides for checks on the suitability of persons working with older children.

Section 79 Amendment of the Children Act 1989

189.   *Section 79(1)* inserts a new Part XA into the Children Act 1989. It will apply to England and Wales, whilst the existing Part X will continue to apply to Scotland. The notes below refer to the new sections 79A to 79W to be inserted into the Children Act by section 79. Throughout the notes on this Part, the term 'registration authority' means HMCIS in relation to England, and the National Assembly in relation to Wales.

Introductory

Section 79A Child minders and day care providers

190.   This section defines the child care providers covered by Part XA. A child minder is defined as a person who is paid (by any form of payment, including payment in kind) to look after a child or children under the age of eight on domestic premises. However, nannies who come into the parents' home are excluded from this definition, except where they look after the children of more than two families. Day care is defined as that provided for children aged under eight in places other than domestic premises. For example, care provided in nurseries, crèches, playgroups *etc*. This section also expands on the definition used in Part X of the Children Act to clarify that "day care" covers care provided at any time of the day or night.

191.   In addition, this section applies Part XA only to those providing day care or child minding for more than two hours a day. However, a child minder who works only between 6

pm and 2 am is not required to register under Part XA. This is to prevent certain informal babysitting arrangements from being caught by Part XA.

Section 79B Other definitions, etc.

192.   This section establishes HMCIS (i.e. Ofsted) and the National Assembly as the registration authorities responsible for the regulation of day care and childminding in England and Wales respectively. It sets out the criteria which must be met in order for a person to be qualified to be registered as a child minder or day care provider. The conditions include a requirement for providers and others who may be on the premises (for example, employees or other residents) to be suitable to be with the children. In addition, this section defines "care", "domestic premises" and identifies the "Tribunal" as that established by the Protection of Children Act 1999.

Regulations

Section 79C Regulations etc. governing child minders and day care providers

193.   This section gives the Secretary of State and the National Assembly for Wales powers to make regulations governing registered child minders and day care providers. The Secretary of State has to consult HMCIS and anyone else he considers appropriate before regulations are made. The regulations may cover how providers deliver their services or how HMCIS fulfils his regulatory function. Regulations in Wales will be developed by the Assembly in full consultation with all interested parties, bodies and authorities. A registered child minder or day care provider may be guilty of an offence if they fail, without reasonable excuse, to comply with any regulation requirements. The offence carries a fine of up to level 5 on the standard scale[*].

Registration

Section 79D Requirement to register

194.   This section requires child minders and day care providers to register with HMCIS in order to operate in England, or with the National Assembly in order to operate in Wales. It also empowers, but does not require, the registration authorities to serve an enforcement notice on an unregistered childminder. It is offence to act, without reasonable excuse, as an unregistered childminder whilst the notice is in effect. It is also an offence to act as an unregistered day care provider. Offences under this section will carry a fine of up to level 5 on the standard scale.

---

[*] See paragraph 97 of these notes for definition of standard scale.

Care Standards

2000 Chapter 14 - *continued*

back to previous text

PART VI

CHILD MINDING AND DAY CARE

Amendment of Children Act 1989.

79. - (1) After Part X of the 1989 Act (child minding and day care for young children) there shall be inserted-

"PART XA

CHILD MINDING AND DAY CARE FOR CHILDREN IN ENGLAND AND WALES

Introductory

Child minders and day care providers.

79A. - (1) This section and section 79B apply for the purposes of this Part.

(2) "Act as a child minder" means (subject to the following subsections) look after one or more children under the age of eight on domestic premises for reward; and "child minding" shall be interpreted accordingly.

(3) A person who-

(a) is the parent, or a relative, of a child;

(b) has parental responsibility for a child;

(c) is a local authority foster parent in relation to a child;

(d) is a foster parent with whom a child has been placed by a voluntary organisation; or

(e) fosters a child privately,

does not act as a child minder when looking after that child.

(4) Where a person-

(a) looks after a child for the parents ("P1"), or

(b) in addition to that work, looks after another child for different parents ("P2"),

and the work consists (in a case within paragraph (a)) of looking after the child wholly or mainly in P1's home or (in a case within paragraph (b)) of looking after the children wholly or mainly in P1's home or P2's home or both, the work is not to be treated as child minding.

(5) In subsection (4), "parent", in relation to a child, includes-

> (a) a person who is not a parent of the child but who has parental responsibility for the child;
>
> (b) a person who is a relative of the child.

(6) "Day care" means care provided at any time for children under the age of eight on premises other than domestic premises.

(7) This Part does not apply in relation to a person who acts as a child minder, or provides day care on any premises, unless the period, or the total of the periods, in any day which he spends looking after children or (as the case may be) during which the children are looked after on the premises exceeds two hours.

(8) In determining whether a person is required to register under this Part for child minding, any day on which he does not act as a child minder at any time between 2 am and 6 pm is to be disregarded.

Other definitions, etc.

79B. - (1) The registration authority in relation to England is Her Majesty's Chief Inspector of Schools in England (referred to in this Part as the Chief Inspector) and references to the Chief Inspector's area are references to England.

(2) The registration authority in relation to Wales is the National Assembly for Wales (referred to in this Act as "the Assembly").

(3) A person is qualified for registration for child minding if-

> (a) he, and every other person looking after children on any premises on which he is or is likely to be child minding, is suitable to look after children under the age of eight;
>
> (b) every person living or employed on the premises in question is suitable to be in regular contact with children under the age of eight;
>
> (c) the premises in question are suitable to be used for looking after children under the age of eight, having regard to their condition and the condition and appropriateness of any equipment on the premises and to any other factor connected with the situation,

construction or size of the premises; and

(d) he is complying with regulations under section 79C and with any conditions imposed by the registration authority.

(4) A person is qualified for registration for providing day care on particular premises if-

(a) every person looking after children on the premises is suitable to look after children under the age of eight;

(b) every person living or working on the premises is suitable to be in regular contact with children under the age of eight;

(c) the premises are suitable to be used for looking after children under the age of eight, having regard to their condition and the condition and appropriateness of any equipment on the premises and to any other factor connected with the situation, construction or size of the premises; and

(d) he is complying with regulations under section 79C and with any conditions imposed by the registration authority.

(5) For the purposes of subsection (4)(b) a person is not treated as working on the premises in question if-

(a) none of his work is done in the part of the premises in which children are looked after; or

(b) he does not work on the premises at times when children are looked after there.

(6) "Domestic premises" means any premises which are wholly or mainly used as a private dwelling and "premises" includes any area and any vehicle.

(7) "Regulations" means-

(a) in relation to England, regulations made by the Secretary of State;

(b) in relation to Wales, regulations made by the Assembly.

(8) "Tribunal" means the Tribunal established by section 9 of the Protection of Children Act 1999.

(9) Schedule 9A (which supplements the provisions of this Part) shall have effect.

Regulations"

Regulations etc. governing child minders and day care providers.

79C. - (1) The Secretary of State may, after consulting the Chief Inspector and any other person he considers appropriate, make regulations governing the activities of registered persons who act as child minders, or provide day care, on premises in England.

(2) The Assembly may make regulations governing the activities of registered persons who act as child minders, or provide day care, on premises in Wales.

(3) The regulations under this section may deal with the following matters (among others)-

(a) the welfare and development of the children concerned;

(b) suitability to look after, or be in regular contact with, children under the age of eight;

(c) qualifications and training;

(d) the maximum number of children who may be looked after and the number of persons required to assist in looking after them;

(e) the maintenance, safety and suitability of premises and equipment;

(f) the keeping of records;

(g) the provision of information.

(4) In relation to activities on premises in England, the power to make regulations under this section may be exercised so as to confer powers or impose duties on the Chief Inspector in the exercise of his functions under this Part.

(5) In particular they may be exercised so as to require or authorise the Chief Inspector, in exercising those functions, to have regard to or meet factors, standards and other matters prescribed by or referred to in the regulations.

(6) If the regulations require any person (other than the registration authority) to have regard to or meet factors, standards and other matters prescribed by or referred to in the regulations, they may also provide for any allegation that the person has failed to do so to be taken into account-

(a) by the registration authority in the exercise of its functions under this Part, or

(b) in any proceedings under this Part.

(7) Regulations may provide-

(a) that a registered person who without reasonable excuse contravenes, or otherwise fails to comply with, any requirement of the regulations shall be guilty of an offence;

and

(b) that a person guilty of the offence shall be liable on summary conviction to a fine not exceeding level 5 on the standard scale.

Registration

79D. - (1) No person shall-

Requirement to register.

(a) act as a child minder in England unless he is registered under this Part for child minding by the Chief Inspector; or

(b) act as a child minder in Wales unless he is registered under this Part for child minding by the Assembly.

(2) Where it appears to the registration authority that a person has contravened subsection (1), the authority may serve a notice ("an enforcement notice") on him.

(3) An enforcement notice shall have effect for a period of one year beginning with the date on which it is served.

(4) If a person in respect of whom an enforcement notice has effect contravenes subsection (1) without reasonable excuse (whether the contravention occurs in England or Wales), he shall be guilty of an offence.

(5) No person shall provide day care on any premises unless he is registered under this Part for providing day care on those premises by the registration authority.

(6) If any person contravenes subsection (5) without reasonable excuse, he shall be guilty of an offence.

(7) A person guilty of an offence under this section shall be liable on summary conviction to a fine not exceeding level 5 on the standard scale.

Applications for registration.

79E. - (1) A person who wishes to be registered under this Part shall make an application to the registration authority.

(2) The application shall-

(a) give prescribed information about prescribed matters;

(b) give any other information which the registration authority reasonably requires the applicant to give.

(3) Where a person provides, or proposes to provide, day care on different premises, he shall make a separate application in respect of each of them.

(4) Where the registration authority has sent the applicant

notice under section 79L(1) of its intention to refuse an application under this section, the application may not be withdrawn without the consent of the authority.

(5) A person who, in an application under this section, knowingly makes a statement which is false or misleading in a material particular shall be guilty of an offence and liable, on summary conviction, to a fine not exceeding level 5 on the standard scale.

Grant or refusal of registration.

79F. - (1) If, on an application by a person for registration for child minding-

(a) the registration authority is of the opinion that the applicant is, and will continue to be, qualified for registration for child minding (so far as the conditions of section 79B(3) are applicable); and

(b) the applicant pays the prescribed fee,

the authority shall grant the application; otherwise, it shall refuse it.

(2) If, on an application by any person for registration for providing day care on any premises-

(a) the registration authority is of the opinion that the applicant is, and will continue to be, qualified for registration for providing day care on those premises (so far as the conditions of section 79B(4) are applicable); and

(b) the applicant pays the prescribed fee,

the authority shall grant the application; otherwise, it shall refuse it.

(3) An application may, as well as being granted subject to any conditions the authority thinks necessary or expedient for the purpose of giving effect to regulations under section 79C, be granted subject to any other conditions the authority thinks fit to impose.

(4) The registration authority may as it thinks fit vary or remove any condition to which the registration is subject or impose a new condition.

(5) Any register kept by a registration authority of persons who act as child minders or provide day care shall be open to inspection by any person at all reasonable times.

(6) A registered person who without reasonable excuse contravenes, or otherwise fails to comply with, any condition imposed on his registration shall be guilty of an offence.

(7) A person guilty of an offence under subsection (6) shall be liable on summary conviction to a fine not exceeding level 5 on the standard scale.

Cancellation of registration.

79G. - (1) The registration authority may cancel the registration of any person if-

> (a) in the case of a person registered for child minding, the authority is of the opinion that the person has ceased or will cease to be qualified for registration for child minding;

> (b) in the case of a person registered for providing day care on any premises, the authority is of the opinion that the person has ceased or will cease to be qualified for registration for providing day care on those premises,

or if an annual fee which is due from the person has not been paid.

(2) Where a requirement to make any changes or additions to any services, equipment or premises has been imposed on a registered person under section 79F(3), his registration shall not be cancelled on the ground of any defect or insufficiency in the services, equipment or premises if-

> (a) the time set for complying with the requirements has not expired; and

> (b) it is shown that the defect or insufficiency is due to the changes or additions not having been made.

(3) Any cancellation under this section must be in writing.

Suspension of registration.

79H. - (1) Regulations may provide for the registration of any person for acting as a child minder or providing day care to be suspended for a prescribed period by the registration authority in prescribed circumstances.

(2) Any regulations made under this section shall include provision conferring on the person concerned a right of appeal to the Tribunal against suspension.

Resignation of registration.

79J. - (1) A person who is registered for acting as a child minder or providing day care may by notice in writing to the registration authority resign his registration.

(2) But a person may not give a notice under subsection (1)-

> (a) if the registration authority has sent him a notice under section 79L(1) of its intention to cancel the registration, unless the authority has decided not to take that step; or

> (b) if the registration authority has sent him a notice under section 79L(5) of its decision to cancel the registration and

Section 79E Applications for registration
195.   This section provides for the application procedure to be followed by a person wishing to act as a child minder or day care provider. The provision of day care on different premises requires separate applications in respect of each premises.

Section 79F Grant or refusal of registration
196.   This section sets the criteria, including payment of a prescribed fee, to be met in order for the registration authority to register a person as a child minder or day care provider. If a registered child minder or day care provider fails to comply with any of the conditions of registration, they may be liable for a fine of up to level 5 on the standard scale. The authority must also make any register of child minders and day care providers available to the public.

Section 79G Cancellation of registration
197.   This section enables the registration authority to cancel registration if it considers the child minder or day care provider has ceased or will cease to be eligible or if the annual fee has not been paid. Any cancellation must be in writing.

Section 79H Suspension of registration
198.   This section enables regulations to be made which would give the registration authority a power to suspend registration. It is envisaged the power will be exercised when children are considered to be at risk in circumstances which may lead to cancellation of registration. Any regulations made will allow providers a right of appeal to the Tribunal against suspension.

Section 79J Resignation of registration
199.   This section makes new provision for child minders and day care providers to voluntarily give up their registration. This will be helpful, for example, in ensuring that information for parents seeking child care provision relates only to active providers. However, resignation of registration is not permitted in circumstances where cancellation of registration is a possibility.

Section 79K Protection of children in an emergency
200.   This section provides that the registration authority can apply to the Magistrates' court for an emergency order in respect of a registered childminder or day care provider where the registration authority believes that a child in their care is suffering, or is likely to suffer, significant harm. The order may cancel the person's registration, vary or remove a condition of registration, or impose a new condition of registration with immediate effect.

Section 79L Notice of intention to take steps
201.   This section sets out the procedure for notification of decisions by the registration authority. It gives the applicant or registered person a right to make representations about a proposal to take action to which he objects.

Section 79M Appeals

202.   This section enables an appeal to the Tribunal to be made against any decision of the registration authority made under section 79L or an order made under section 79K. The Tribunal may allow or refuse an appeal and may impose, vary or cancel any condition of registration.

Inspection: England

Section 79N General functions of the Chief Inspector

203.   This section imposes duties on HMCIS to provide the Secretary of State with information and advice on registered child minding and day care. He must report on his Part XA functions and on related matters.

Section 70P Early years child care inspectorate

204.   This section requires HMCIS to set up and maintain a register of early years child care inspectors ("registered inspectors"). The register may be combined with Ofsted's existing register of nursery education inspectors to form a single register of all early years inspectors.

Section 79Q Inspection of provision of child minding and day care in England

205.   This section provides that child minding and day care inspections are to be carried out by registered early years child care inspectors. Inspections are to be carried out at intervals set out in regulations. HMCIS may either organise inspections or arrange with others for them to organise inspections (for example, by contracting out the work). The registered inspector is required to report on the inspections carried out under this section.

Section 79R Reports of inspections

206.   This section requires registered inspectors to produce written reports on inspections they carry out for HMCIS within a prescribed time limit. Reports are sent to the Secretary of State and may also be made available to other prescribed people. HMCIS has a power to edit reports where appropriate (for example, to preserve confidentiality).

Inspection: Wales

207.   In general no provision is made for the Assembly to prescribe the detailed arrangements for inspection on the face of the Act. As consistent with other parts of the Act a power to enable inspections to be undertaken is sufficient for Wales. Detailed matters of inspection such as this will be dealt with through existing powers of the National Assembly. Under the Act, Estyn (the Welsh equivalent of Ofsted) will be able to become involved in inspections of premises subject to the provisions of Part VI.

Section 79S General functions of the Assembly

208.   *Subsection (1)* provides for the Assembly to provide training to assist day care providers and childminders. *Subsection (2)* provides a parallel power to that in section 79N (5) so that the Assembly may, by regulation, confer additional functions on itself, but only where that function has already been conferred on HMCIS by the Secretary of State.

Section 79T Inspection: Wales

209.   *Subsection (1)* provides a parallel power to that in section 79N (2) so that the Assembly can require a registered person in Wales to provide any information the Assembly considers necessary to carry out its functions. *Subsection (2)* provides regulation-making powers in respect of inspecting the quality and standards of day care and childminding and in publishing reports of inspections. *Subsection (3)* enables the Assembly to organise inspections or make arrangements with Estyn or others to organise the inspections.

210.   The National Assembly will employ inspectors directly and will not need to create a register of inspectors for any of its responsibilities under this Part .

Supplementary

Section 79U Rights of entry etc. in England

211.   This section gives registered inspectors powers of entry to any premises on which child minding or day care is provided. Entry may be gained for general inspection purposes or where an inspector reasonably believes a child may be at risk. It is an offence carrying a fine of up to level 4 on the standard scale to obstruct an inspector exercising his powers under this section.

Section 79V Function of local authorities

212.   This section provides that, in accordance with regulations, local authorities will provide information, training and advice on child minding and day care provision.

Checks on suitability of persons working with children over the age of seven

Section 79W Requirement for certificate of suitability

213.   This section enables regulations to be made to place duties, if certain conditions are met, on those who provide care for children aged eight and over for more than five hours a

week, and who would otherwise not have to register under Part XA. Providers are required to hold a valid certificate for themselves and others on the premises (for example, employees or other residents) which demonstrates to parents that they are suitable to look after children. The regulations under this section may create certain offences in connection with the certificate. These will carry a fine of up to level 5 on the standard scale.

214.   *Section 79(2)* gives effect to *Schedule 3*, which inserts a new Schedule 9A into the Children Act 1989 (see below). Section 79 (3) and (4) enable an order to be made setting out the scheme to transfer staff currently working for local authorities to the regulatory authority. Section 79(5) disapplies Part X of the Children Act in England and Wales. It will continue to apply in Scotland.

Schedule 3 Child Minding and Day Care for Young Children
215.   *Paragraphs 1, 2 and 3* disapply certain schools or other establishments from Part XA. This means they need not be registered by the registration authority, although regulation making powers may require some schools to register in certain circumstances. Hospitals which care for children as patients are to be excluded from regulation, although on site child care provision (for example, a crèche for the children of staff), will be regulated. Premises which are used for day care for less than six days a year are exempted.

216.   *Paragraph 4* provides for regulations to be made as to the circumstances in which a person can be disqualified from registering as a child minder or day care provider or from otherwise being involved in the provision of day care. The precise grounds for disqualification will be set out in regulations. These provisions also apply to members of the household, potential employees and managers of day care businesses.

217.   *Paragraph 5* provides that contravention of the provision made by or under paragraph 4 is an offence unless one of the defences set out in *subparagraphs (2)* or *(3)* applies. The penalty for this offence is up to 6 months imprisonment, a fine not exceeding level 5 on the standard scale or both.

218.   *Paragraph 6* provides for certificates of registration to be issued to successful applicants. *Paragraph 7* provides for regulations to be made requiring registered childminders and day care providers to pay an annual fee to the registration authority. *Paragraph 8* enables the registration authority to ask for and receive assistance from local authorities in carrying out its child minding and day care regulatory duties.

PART VII: PROTECTION OF CHILDREN AND VULNERABLE ADULTS

Protection of vulnerable adults

219.   **Part VII** introduces provisions by which the Secretary of State will establish and operate, in relation to both England and Wales, a list of persons who are considered unsuitable to work with vulnerable adults. Providers of care services, including care homes, domiciliary care agencies and prescribed services within both NHS and independent healthcare settings will be required to refer individuals for inclusion in the list *(section 82)*. Provision is also made for registration authorities to refer individuals for inclusion in both the list kept under section 1 of the Protection of Children Act 1999 (PoCA) and the list kept under this Part (PoVA), *(sections 84 and 95)*, and for referrals to be made as a result of certain inquiries. *(Sections 85 and 96)*. *Section 89* places a duty on providers of care services to vulnerable adults to check that prospective employees are not on the list, and to refuse employment in that field to any person included on the list. They must also stop employing a person in a care position if they discover they are on the appropriate list. A person who seeks work in a care position while they are confirmed on the list commits an offence.

220.   Individuals will have a right of appeal against a decision to include them on the list, and will be able to apply to have their name removed from the list after ten years (five years if aged under 18 at the time their listing was confirmed *(sections 86 - 88)*. Provision is also made for cross-referrals between this list and the list of persons considered unsuitable to work with children established under section 1 of PoCA, and *vice versa (sections 92 and 97)*. Further amendments are made to the Education Act 1986 such that persons who are unsuitable to work with children are disqualified from working in independent schools.

Section 80 Basic definitions

221.   This section provides the basic definitions relevant to this Part of the Act. *Subsection (2)* defines care workers. Broadly, these are individuals employed in care homes, private and voluntary hospitals or clinics, independent medical agencies or NHS establishments who have regular contact with vulnerable adults in the course of their normal duties, and individuals who provide personal care to people in their own homes. The approach for healthcare establishments is that these provisions will only apply where individuals are employed in prescribed services. For example, staff on a geriatric ward would be included, but staff on a paediatric ward would not be. *Subsection (3)* defines "care position".

222.   *Subsection (4)* provides that for this Part of the Act, employment is defined as it is in section 12(1) of PoCA:

"employment"-

(a)   means any employment, whether paid or unpaid and whether under a contract of service or apprenticeship, under a contract for services, or otherwise than under a contract; and
(b)   includes an office established by or by virtue of a prescribed enactment,

and references to an individual being employed shall be construed accordingly.

223.   *Subsection (5)* defines supply workers. These are workers who are found care work through employment agencies or businesses, including those supplied by domiciliary care agencies to provide personal care to people in their own homes. The definition also includes temporary staff supplied by employment agencies or businesses to work in care positions as defined in subsection (3).

224.   *Subsection (6)* defines vulnerable adults. Three groups of adults are identified:

- those receiving accommodation and nursing or personal care in a care home;
- those receiving personal care in their own home through a domiciliary care agency; and
- those receiving certain services in healthcare settings, including private, voluntary and NHS establishments. (The services included will be set out in regulations under subsection (2) above).

225.   *Subsection (7)* defines the providers of services to vulnerable adults. These are any person who is registered as carrying on a care home, a domiciliary care agency, or an independent healthcare establishment, independent medical agency or NHS body which provides prescribed services.

226.   *Subsection (8)* The PoVA scheme will be operated by the Secretary of State for both England and Wales, but with the Secretary of State alone having regulation making powers. However, he will be required to consult the National Assembly for Wales before making any such regulations.

Section 81 Duty of Secretary of State to keep list
227.   *Section 81* places a duty on the Secretary of State to keep a list of individuals who are considered unsuitable to work with vulnerable adults. The list will be kept by the Secretary of State for Health in relation to both England and Wales. A person can only be included on the list if he has been referred to the Secretary of State in accordance with the provisions of this Part. *Subsection (3)* enables the Secretary of State to remove a person from the list should he be satisfied that they should not have been included on it in the first instance.

Section 82 Persons who provide care for vulnerable adults: duty to refer
228.   *Section 82* sets out the duty on providers of care services for vulnerable adults to refer care workers to the Secretary of State for inclusion in the list under certain circumstances. The circumstances, set out in *subsection (2)*, turn on a worker having placed a protected adult

at risk of harm, whether or not in the course of his employment. The circumstances include not only that a worker has been dismissed on grounds of misconduct which harmed or risked harm to a vulnerable adult, but that a worker has resigned or retired before the employer has dismissed him; that they have been transferred to other work; that they have been suspended or provisionally transferred to other duties pending a final decision of the employer; or that they have been made redundant in circumstances where the employer would otherwise have considered dismissing them. The definition of "harm" is given in *section 121* (General interpretation *etc*).

229. *Subsection (3)* further provides that if, after a worker has resigned, retired, been dismissed or been transferred to other duties, relevant information comes to light, the employer is still under a duty to refer the person to the Secretary of State for inclusion on the list.

230. *Subsections (4)* to *(7)* describe the process that the Secretary of State must use to determine whether a referred person should be included on the list. Providing that the Secretary of State considers it may be appropriate to list the person, then the person will be provisionally included in the list while the referral is under consideration. The Secretary of State will invite both the person referred and the provider to make any observations on the information the other submits, and if he thinks appropriate, will subsequently invite each to comment on the other party's observations. The Secretary of State will come to a decision once all the relevant information has been received, and he has been notified that any pending action against the worker has resulted in dismissal or permanent transfer to other duties. If the Secretary of State forms the opinion that it was reasonable for the provider to consider the care worker guilty of misconduct, and that the person is unsuitable to work with vulnerable adults, then the person's name will be confirmed on the list.

231. *Subsection (10)* makes it clear that referrals are not required unless the dismissal, resignation *etc.* occurred after the commencement of this section. This is a similar approach to that adopted under PoCA, section 2(10).

Section 83 Employment agencies and businesses: duty to refer
232. Employment agencies and businesses are similarly required to refer supply workers to the list under appropriate circumstances. Under *subsection (2),* an employment agency must make a referral where it has decided not to do any further business with the worker on the grounds of misconduct which harmed a vulnerable adult or placed him or her at risk of harm; or where on those grounds has decided not to find them any further employment as a supply worker. An employment business must refer where it has dismissed a supply worker on the grounds of misconduct which harmed, etc, a vulnerable adult; where the supply worker has retired or resigned but otherwise the employment business would have dismissed or considered dismissing him on those grounds; or where on those grounds it has decided not to supply him for further work in a care position *(subsection (3))*. The procedure the Secretary of State must follow after a referral is similar to that set out in section 82. Again, there is no requirement to refer in cases where the dismissal, resignation *etc.*, or decision no longer to

provide or supply the worker to fill a care position occurred before this section comes into force.

Section 84 Power of registration authority to refer

233.   *Section 84* gives the registration authority (in England the Commission; in Wales the Assembly), the power to refer worker to the Secretary of State that they consider guilty of misconduct. This section enables the registration authorities to make referrals when they come across evidence of misconduct in the course of their inspections that has not been referred to the Secretary of State by the employer. This power would be used in cases where employers have not fulfilled the responsibilities Part VII places on them to refer workers who have caused harm, or risked harm to vulnerable adults. Such circumstances could occur when a care home has been closed and the owner is refusing to co-operate or in small establishments where the owner may be directly involved in care provision, has caused harm himself and has not referred himself.

Section 85 Individuals named in the findings of certain inquiries

234.   This section provides for the Secretary of State to be able to consider for inclusion on the list individuals who have been named in the findings of certain inquiries. It also describes the process that the Secretary of State must use to determine whether a person so named should be included on the list. If it appears to the Secretary of State that the person who held the inquiry found that the individual was guilty of relevant misconduct while employed in a care position and that the individual is unsuitable to work with vulnerable adults then the person will be provisionally included in the list. The Secretary of State will invite observations from the individual on the report, so far as it relates to him, and from the employer of the individual at the time the misconduct took place. If he feels it is appropriate, the Secretary of State will invite each to comment on the other party's observations. The Secretary of State will come to a decision once all the relevant information has been received.

235.   *Subsection (6)* defines "relevant employer" and "relevant misconduct". *Subsections (7)* to *(9)* provide a list of relevant inquiries to which this section may apply, and provides the Secretary of State with an order making power (in consultation with the Assembly), to add other inquiries or hearings to this list.

Section 86 Appeals against inclusion in the list

236.   Individuals will have a right to appeal against a decision by Secretary of State to include them on the list, but (subject to *subsection (2)*) not against a provisional inclusion while the referral is being investigated. Appeals will be heard by the Tribunal established under PoCA. Individuals will also be able to apply to the Tribunal to appeal against a decision of the Secretary of State not to remove their name from the list on the grounds that their inclusion was erroneous.

237.   If the Tribunal is not satisfied, either that the individual was guilty of misconduct, or that he is unsuitable to work with vulnerable adults, it will allow the appeal and direct that the individual's name should be removed from the list. In considering an appeal where an

individual has been convicted of an offence, the Tribunal cannot challenge any fact on which the conviction was based.

238. *Subsection (2)* provides that if an individual's name has provisionally been on the list for more than nine months without a decision being made, he can ask the Tribunal to determine his case instead of the Secretary of State. This will not apply where a criminal or civil case is pending, in which case the individual cannot ask the Tribunal to determine his case until 6 months after the final outcome (or "final determination") of the court case. "Final determination" is defined in *subsection (6)*.

Section 87 Applications for removal from the list

239. Under this section, individuals are given a right to apply to have their name removed from the list once a period of ten years has elapsed. Applications will be made to the Tribunal, as before, and it will be for the Tribunal to determine whether the individual is still unsuitable to work with vulnerable adults.

Section 88 Conditions for application under section 87

240. *Section 88* gives conditions for application for removal from the list. It provides that such applications may only be made with leave of the tribunal. An individual may only apply after he has been permanently listed for at least ten years, and if unsuccessful, at ten yearly intervals after that. Anyone who was aged under 18 at the time of permanent listing can apply to have his name removed after five years (and at five yearly intervals after that). It will be for the Tribunal to determine whether an individual is now suitable to work with vulnerable adults.

Section 89 Effect of inclusion in list

241. This section places a duty on providers of care services to vulnerable adults, including domiciliary care agencies, to check that prospective employees are not on the list before offering them employment in a care position. If they do find the person is on the list, they must not employ them in a care position. Where workers are being supplied by an employment agency or business, the provider may instead obtain written confirmation from the agency or business to the effect that they have checked that the individual is not on the list within the last twelve months. Should an employer discover that an employee is listed then they are obliged to stop employing them in a care position.

242. *Subsection (5)* makes it an offence for a person confirmed on the list to apply for, accept or do any work in a care position. A person committing an offence under this subsection would be liable on conviction in the Magistrate's Court to imprisonment for up to six months, and a fine of up to £5000 (level five on the standard scale); and in the Crown Court to imprisonment for up to five years and an unlimited fine. It will be a defence for a listed person charged with an offence under this subsection to prove that they did not know, and could not reasonably be expected to know, that they were on the list.

Section 90   Searches of list under Part V of Police Act 1997

243.   *Section 90* amends section 113 and 115 of the Police Act 1997. These amendments will, when commenced, enable the Criminal Records Bureau to supply an individual with a criminal record certificate or enhanced criminal record certificate which states whether he is included on the list, and gives any details of the inclusion as may be required in regulations.

Section 91   Access to list before commencement of section 90

244.   This section provides that pending such time as the Criminal Records Bureau takes on the function of issuing criminal record certificates, any person who wishes to offer an individual employment in a care position, or an employment agency or domiciliary care agency who wishes to take on an individual, or any other person as may be defined in regulations, is entitled on application to the Secretary of State to the information as to whether the individual is on the list. An application can still be made if the individual is already employed by the person. This means, for example, that an employer can carry out a check in order for a person to change their duties and work in a care position when they had not done so before.

Section 92   Persons referred for inclusion in list under Protection of Children Act 1999

245.   This section deals with cross-referrals between this list and the list established under section 1 of PoCA, which lists individuals considered unsuitable to work with children. Where a person is referred under PoCA but it appears from the alleged misconduct that they may be unsuitable to work with vulnerable adults, it provides a mechanism for considering inclusion on the PoVA list. *Subsection (3)* provides, however, that a person can only be provisionally included in, or have his inclusion confirmed in, the PoVA list, if he is also included in the PoCA list.

Section 93   Power to extend Part VII

246.   *Section 93* gives the Secretary of State the power to make regulations to make changes to the list in section 80(7) defining persons providing care to vulnerable adults, and to amend the definitions given in section 80 of "care worker", "care position" and "vulnerable adult". Section 93 gives the Secretary of State power to amend the definitions in section 80 so as to bring within the scope of Part VII any social services provided by local authorities or others, and health services outside the NHS.

247.   The section allows the Secretary of State to keep the coverage of Part VII up to date, for example, should the scope of services regulated under Part II of the Act be altered in the future. The power to extend will also enable the coverage of Part VII to be kept relevant to changing patterns of service delivery. For example, it is intended that day centres will be brought within the range of services regulated under Part II of this Act in the foreseeable future. This section would enable the Secretary of State to extend the provisions of Part VII to include care workers in day centre services.

The List kept under Section 1 of the 1999 Act

248. *Sections 94* to *104* make necessary amendments to PoCA.

Section 94 Employment agencies and businesses
249.   This section inserts a new section into PoCA to modify the application of that Act to employment businesses.

Section 95 Inclusion in 1999 Act list on reference by certain authorities
250.   *Section 95* provides analogous powers to section 84 by amending PoCA to allow the Commission, the Assembly and Her Majesty's Chief Inspector of Schools in England to refer child care workers to the Secretary of State. This power would be used when these bodies, in the course of their duties, come across child care workers who they consider to be guilty of misconduct which has harmed, or risked harm to children and who have not been referred to the Secretary of State by their employers. This misconduct need not necessarily be committed in the course of their employment. This power would be used, for example, in cases where employers, for whatever reason, had not fulfilled their responsibilities under PoCA, to refer workers guilty of misconduct to the Secretary of State.

Section 96 Inclusion in 1999 Act list of individuals named in findings of certain inquiries
251.   This section is exactly analogous to section 85. It amends section 2A of PoCA and provides for the Secretary of State to be able to consider for inclusion on the list, individuals who have been named in the findings of certain inquiries. It also describes the process that the Secretary of State must use to determine whether a person so named should be included on the list. If it appears to the Secretary of State that the person who held the inquiry found that the individual was guilty of relevant misconduct while in a child care position and that the individual is unsuitable to work with children then the person will be provisionally included in the List. The Secretary of State will invite observations from the individual on the report, so far as it relates to him, and from the employer of the individual at the time the misconduct took place. If he feels it is appropriate, the Secretary of State will invite each to comment on the other party's observations. The Secretary of State will come to a decision once all the relevant information has been received.

252.   *Subsection (6)* defines "relevant employer" and "relevant misconduct". *Subsections (7)* to *(9)* provide a list of relevant types of inquiry, and provide the Secretary of State with an order making power (in consultation with the Assembly), to enable him to add other types of inquiries or hearings to this list.

Section 97 Inclusion in 1999 Act on reference under this Part
253.   This section inserts a new section 3A into PoCA to take account of cross-referral matters. It mirrors the provision under section 92, in that the Secretary of State may in some circumstances consider an individual for inclusion in the PoCA list when they have been

referred for inclusion in the PoVA list, but only if he also includes the person in the PoVA list.

Section 98 Individuals providing care funded by direct payments

254.   *Section 98* extends the provisions of PoCA to child care workers employed through certain direct payments. *Subsection (1)* enables a local authority to refer to the PoCA list a relevant individual whom the authority considers is guilty of misconduct which harmed a child or placed a child at risk of harm. "Relevant individual" is defined as a person who is or has been employed to provide care to a child, where that employment is funded by a direct payment under section 17A of the Children Act.

255.   *Subsections (2)* and *(3)* amend PoCA so as to require a local authority to check whether an individual is in the list before making a direct payment, if the parent proposing to employ the individual asks it to. Regulations made under *section 103* will permit these checks to be made pending the coming into operation of the Criminal Records Bureau.

Section 99   Transfer from Consultancy Service Index of individuals named in past inquiries

256.   This section amends section 3 of PoCA. It enables names held on the Consultancy Service Index as a result of a relevant inquiry, to be transferred to the Protection of Children Act list in circumstances where it appears to the Secretary of State that the person who held the inquiry found the individual guilty of misconduct, and that the individual is unsuitable to work with children.

Restrictions on working with children in independent schools

Section 100 Additional ground of complaint

257.   *Section 100* amends the Education Act 1996 so as to provide for the disqualification from working in an independent school of persons who are unsuitable to work with children. A right of appeal to an Independent Schools Tribunal is given in *subsection (2)* against a proposal by the Secretary of State to disqualify a person on those grounds.

Section 101 Effect of inclusion in 1996 Act list

258.   *Section 101* amends PoCA so as to require child care organisations, when proposing to offer employment in a child care position, to check that the person they are intending to take on is not disqualified from working in independent schools on those grounds. If he is, they are prohibited from taking him on in that position.

Section 102 Searches of 1996 Act list

259.   It is intended that, when Part V of the Police Act 1997, which provides for the Criminal Records Bureau, comes into force, checks against the exclusion list established under PoCA can be made through that mechanism. *Section 102* makes amendments to the Police Act 1997 to enable the checks provided for in the sections 100 and 101 above, to be made under the provisions of Part V of the Police Act when it comes into force.

General

Section 103 Temporary provision for access to lists

260. This section replaces sections 13(3) and 13(4) of PoCA to take account of amendments made by this Act. It ensures that all relevant lists can be accessed by all relevant organisations in advance of the establishment of the Criminal Records Bureau. *Subsection (1)* identifies the lists that the amendment is concerned with, and *subsection (2)* defines who may access the lists under these interim arrangements. This subsection also provides a power to make regulations broadening the range of organisations that will have access to the lists during this interim period, and similarly widens the range of positions in respect of which they will be able to make checks. Thus, for example, it will allow regulations to be made which will allow adoption societies access to the lists when considering the suitability of prospective adoptive parents before *section 104* is commenced.

Section 104 Suitability to adopt a child: searches of lists

261. This section amends sections 113 and 115 of the Police Act 1997, to provide for certain persons to be subject to criminal records checks, and enhanced criminal records[*] checks respectively. In the case of prospective adoptive parents, the enhanced criminal records certificates are to be made available to the local authority or voluntary adoption agency that is carrying out the assessment of a person's suitability to adopt.

262. This section also amends sections 113 and 115 of the Police Act 1997 such that persons who are applying for registration under Part II of this Act (persons carrying on or managing establishments or agencies) and persons applying to be admitted to the registers of social care workers held by the Councils under section 56 of this Act may also be subject to both types of check. For persons applying to be registered under Part VI (childminders and day centre providers), of this Act provisions in *Schedule 4, paragraph 25* make the appropriate amendments to the Police Act 1997.

---

[*] The Police Act 1997 provides for the issue of three types of certificates:

- Criminal Conviction Certificate under section 112. These will just give information about criminal convictions

- Criminal Record Certificate under section 113. These will give information about criminal convictions and cautions, plus information about PoCA/PoVA listing

- Enhanced Criminal Records Certificare under section 115. These will give information about criminal convictions, PoCA/PoVA listing, and in addition, will give such information relating to a persons arrests, or charges and investigations relating to them, which have not led to a conviction or caution and which the relevant chief constable thinks are relevant.

PART VIII MISCELLANEOUS

263.   **Part VIII** imposes a duty on the proprietor of any boarding school or further education colleges with accommodation to safeguard and promote the welfare of any children accommodated there. It empowers the registration authority to inspect the school or college and report on the welfare arrangements for the children there. Section 87 of the Children Act 1989 (which this Part amends), currently makes similar provision in relation to independent boarding schools only. The new requirements will apply to all types of boarding school and further education college, both state and independent sector. *Sections 105 to 110* amend the Children Act 1989. Unless otherwise stated, functions conferred on the Secretary of State in these sections are exercised in Wales by the National Assembly for Wales, and the term "appropriate authority" means, in relation to England, the Commission, and in relation to Wales, the Assembly.

264.   Part VIII also makes new arrangements for the regulation of nurses agencies by removing their exemption from the Employment Agencies Act 1973 and repealing the Nurses Agencies Act 1957; and makes new provision for statutory guidance to be issued to local authorities in respect of charges for home care services.

Boarding Schools and Colleges

Section 105 Welfare of children in boarding schools and colleges
265.   This section extends section 87 of the Children Act (welfare of children in independent schools), to all schools and further education colleges with boarding provision, and puts the duty to monitor welfare in schools onto the appropriate authority in place of the local authority. It imposes a duty upon proprietors and governing bodies to ensure that effective arrangements for the welfare of all children accommodated at boarding schools and colleges are in place and properly adhered to.

266.   The appropriate authority is required to determine whether this duty is being adequately discharged and may carry out inspections for that purpose. Where the appropriate authority determines that a school or college is failing in its duty in respect of the welfare of children it must inform the local education authority, or in England the Secretary of State, as the case may be, for any appropriate enforcement action to be taken in accordance with education legislation. In Wales, the National Assembly will be responsible both for inspection and for any enforcement actions which would, in England, be undertaken by the Secretary of State. By existing section 87(9) of the Children Act, which is not reproduced in the Act, it is an offence to obstruct a person exercising powers of inspection under this section or regulations made under it.

Section 106 Suspension of duty under section 87(3) of the 1989 Act

267.   This section amends sections 87A and 87B of the Children Act as inserted under the provisions of the Deregulation and Contracting Out Act 1994.   Sections 87A and 87B empower the Secretary of State (or in Wales, the Assembly) to appoint a body, which already acts as an inspector of independent boarding schools for other purposes, to undertake the welfare inspection functions conferred by section 87, and allow schools to make inspection arrangements with such substitute inspectors.

268.   The effect of the amendments is to apply these provisions to all boarding schools and further education colleges. Any school or college may enter into an agreement with such a body to inspect its welfare arrangements. The substitute inspector must notify the appropriate authority of its appointment.   In that case, the authority's duty to ensure the welfare of children accommodated at that school or college is suspended until the appointment is terminated or the agreement comes to an end.

Section 107 Boarding schools: national minimum standards

269.   This section inserts a new section 87C making provision for national minimum standards that schools and colleges accommodating children must comply with in relation to the welfare of children. The national minimum standards will be taken into account by the appropriate authority or any substitute inspector in considering whether there has been a failure to safeguard and promote a child's welfare in any school or college, and in any related proceedings. The Secretary of State must undertake a consultation exercise before issuing or substantially amending any standards.

Section 108 Annual fee for boarding school inspections

270.   This section inserts new section 87D which provides for regulations to be made regarding annual inspection fees payable to the appropriate authority. The level of such fees and when they become due will be set out in the regulations. Unpaid fees may be recovered in the Magistrate's court.

Section 109 Inspection of schools etc. by persons authorised by Secretary of State

271.   The Secretary of State and the Assembly (by virtue of section 80(1) of the Children Act) have wide powers to inspect premises in which children are accommodated, including independent schools. This section extends powers under section 80 to inspect or to obtain information, to any school or college providing accommodation for any child. It also adds a person carrying on a fostering agency (as defined in section 4(4)) to those persons whom section 80(5) places under a duty to provide the Secretary of State (or in Wales, the National Assembly) with information or access to records for inspection purposes.

Fostering

Section 110 Extension of Part IX to school children during holidays
272.   The effect of this section is to apply existing provision, whereby a child who stays at an independent boarding school for more than two weeks in the school holidays is treated as a privately fostered child, to all schools. The local authority must be notified of the child's presence in the school and has to satisfy itself as to his welfare.

Employment Agencies

Section 111 Nurses Agencies
273.   This section repeals the Nurses Agencies Act 1957 and brings nurses agencies under the Employment Agencies Act 1973. Nurses agencies are currently licensed by local authorities under the Nurses Agencies Act 1957, while all other employment agencies and businesses are covered by the Employment Agencies Act 1973. The effect of this section is to bring nurses agencies into line with all other types of employment agencies and businesses. In addition, the Government has decided that nurses agencies should be required to register with the Commission (or, for agencies in Wales, the Assembly). (See notes to section 4(5))

274.   These changes apply to England and Wales. Nurses agencies in Scotland will continue to be licensed under Part III of the Nurses (Scotland) Act 1951.

Charges for local authority welfare services

Section 112 Charges for local authority welfare services
275.   Under *Section 112* the powers of local authorities to charge for certain non-residential social services are to be treated as social services functions as defined in the Local Authority Social Services Act 1970 ("LASS Act"). This will allow statutory guidance to be issued under section 7 of the LASS Act for charges for non-residential services. The need to produce statutory guidance follows the publication of the White Paper "Modernising Social Services". This recognised that the scale of variation in local authorities' home care charges was unacceptable. The Audit Commission report "Charging with Care", which was published on 10 May 2000, highlighted the full extent of these variations.

PART IX AND SCHEDULES 4, 5 AND 6: GENERAL AND SUPPLEMENTAL

Chapter I: General

Section 113 Default powers of the appropriate Minister

276.   *Subsection (1)* confers default powers on the Secretary of State in respect of the Commission and the General Social Care Council (GSCC). *Subsection (2)* makes similar provision for default powers for the National Assembly for Wales in respect of the Care Council for Wales (CCW). If the appropriate Minister is satisfied that the Commission or the GSCC or the CCW has failed to discharge any of its functions, without good reason, or in discharging its functions has failed to comply with any directions or guidance given to it, this section confers a two-fold default power.

277.   *Subsection (3)* details the first stage: the appropriate Minister may make an order declaring the Commission or Council to be in default and issue directions requiring them to take specific action within a specific timescale. If the Commission or Council fail to comply with the directions, the second stage *(subsection (4))* is triggered. This results in the appropriate Minister either carrying out the functions himself or nominating a person or organisation to discharge these functions on his behalf.

Section 114 Schemes for transfer of staff

278.   This section provides that the provisions in both this section and *section 94* apply to all transfers of staff made under the Act (see sections 38, 70 and 79(3)). *Subsection (3)* provides that schemes may be made, provided that prescribed requirements for consultation have been met in respect of every individual to be transferred.

Section 115 Effect of schemes

279.   This section provides that all staff transfers made under the Act will reflect the Transfer of Undertakings (Protection of Employment) Regulations 1981 (SI 1981 No 1794) (TUPE) principle, that staff transferred will do so on their existing terms and conditions. In addition, the new bodies may make provision for occupational pensions and compensation for loss of employment. It is intended that staff who transfer will continue to have pension provision through their existing schemes.

280.   *Subsection (1)* provides that under a scheme an employee's existing contract of employment would not be terminated, but would transfer to the new employer and be treated as having effect from the date it was originally made.

281.   *Subsections (3)* and *(4)* provide that an employee may object to transferring to a new employer, and that their contract of employment can be terminated before the date of transfer. This would not be treated as a dismissal.

282.   *Subsection (5)* provides that these arrangements will not affect the right of an employee to terminate his or her contract if their working conditions were to suffer a significant change which was to their detriment.

Section 116 and Schedule 4 Minor and consequential amendments
283.   *Section 116* makes provision for *Schedule 4*, which makes minor and consequential amendments other legislation. The following amendments are of particular note:

284.   *Paragraph 5* amends the Adoption Act 1976 to provide for the regulation of voluntary adoption agencies under this Act.

285.   *Paragraph 14* makes amendments to the Children Act 1989, in particular to the definition of "registered children's home", which becomes a "private children's home" in order to avoid confusion. An "appropriate children's home" is any type of children's home (that is, private, voluntary or community home), in respect of which a person is registered under the Care Standards Act.

286.   *Paragraph 26(3)* amends section 9(2) of the Protection of Children Act 1999 in order that the Tribunal established under that Act should also determine appeals against decisions made under this Act.

Section 117 and Schedules 5 and 6: Transitional provisions, savings and repeals
287.   *Section 117* makes provision for *Schedule 5*, which details transitional provisions and savings, and *Schedule 6* which details repeals.

Schedule 5 Transitional provisions and savings
288.   Limited transitional provision has been made in *Schedule 5* for fostering agencies, voluntary adoption agencies and the Children's Commissioner for Wales. Further transitional provisions will be required in respect the other elements of this Act. This will be dealt with by Order under *section 119*.

Schedule 6 Repeals
289.   *Schedule 6* details repeals.

Chapter II: Supplemental

Section 118 Orders and regulations
290.   *Section 118* provides that all orders and regulations made under the Act, other than certain orders making staff transfer schemes, will be made by statutory instrument. Apart from commencement orders, in England these will be subject to Parliamentary scrutiny under

negative procedures. The Government of Wales Act 1998 places duties on the National Assembly for Wales in respect of making regulations. These are set out in full in Standing Order 22 of the Assembly. An order made by the Secretary of State under section 119(2) which amends the text of an Act is subject to Parliamentary scrutiny under the affirmative procedure. Although the Secretary of State and the Assembly can make regulations independently under this Act, they can also act jointly if they so wish.

291.   *Subsection (5)* gives the appropriate Minister power to use any regulation making power flexibly to make similar or different provision for various cases. For example, in section 22 a power is given to set out in regulations what constitutes 'fit premises'. Different requirements will need to be set depending on whether the premises are to be used as a home, an agency, or another type of registrable establishment.

Section 119 Supplementary and consequential provision *etc.*
292.   *Section 119* gives the appropriate Minister power enabling him to make such additional provision as he considers necessary in order to give full effect to the provisions of the Act.

Section 120 Wales
293.   *Section 120* provides for receipts to the Assembly from registration and other fees to be paid into its own budget rather than the Consolidated Fund.

Section 121 General Interpretation etc.
294.   *Section 121* is a general interpretation provision.

Section 122 Commencement and Section 123 Short title and extent
295.   *Section 122* makes standard provision for commencement. *Section 123* provides that this Act extends only to England and Wales, except section 70 (abolition of CCETSW), which also extends to Scotland and Northern Ireland. In addition, sections 114 and 115 (which relate to schemes for the transfer of staff) and 118 (concerning orders and regulations) also apply to Scotland and Northern Ireland in so far as they relate to staff transfers from CCETSW or the winding-up of CCETSW. Amendments or repeals of any enactments extending to Scotland or Northern Ireland will also extend to those countries.

COMMENCEMENT

296.   The provisions of the Act will come into force on one or more dates.   The commencement order power allows for separate commencement dates in England and Wales but the intention is for the provisions to be commenced in England and Wales at the same time to enable a smooth transfer of responsibilities.

297.   Sections relating to interim arrangements for small children's homes (section 40) and dentists who carry out procedures under general anaesthesia (section 39) will come into force at the earliest opportunity after Royal Assent.   It is envisaged that the provisions relating to the General Social Care Council will be in force in October 2001, with the exception of the register of social care staff. Full details for the register will be developed by the GSCC itself and come into force during 2002 at the earliest.   It is intended that the National Care Standards Commission will be established in 'shadow' form in April 2001, and will begin its registration functions in April 2002.   Functions of Her Majesty's Chief Inspector of Schools will be in force from September 2001, with the exceptions of provisions in section 79W, which will require suitability checks of people caring for over 7s.   These will come into force at a later date.   Decisions on commencement in Wales are for the National Assembly to take but are expected to follow a similar timetable as in England.

DETAILS OF THE BILL'S PASSAGE THROUGH PARLIAMENT ARE AS FOLLOWS:

House of Lords	Date	House of Lords Hansard
Introduction	2 December 1999	Vol 607, Col 916
Second Reading	13 December 1999	Vol 608 Cols 11 – 20 and 34 – 80
Committee	10, 13 and 18 January 2000	Vol 608 Cols 403 – 421 and 434 – 470 Cols 788 – 821 and 834 – 866 Cols 1019 – 1048 and 1067 - 1108
Report	28 March 2000	Vol 611 Cols 643 – 716 and 731 - 798
Third Reading	4 April 2000	Vol 611 Cols 1202 – 1232
Consideration of Commons' Amendments	18 July 2000	Vol 615 Cols 921 - 1002

House of Commons	Date	House of Commons Hansard
Brought from House of Lords	5 April 2000	
Second Reading	18 May 2000	Vol 350 Cols 481 – 563
Committee	25 May – 4 July 2000	Hansard Standing Committee G
Report and Third Reading	12 July 2000	Vol 353 Cols 878 - 1035

Royal Assent	20 July 2000	House of Lords Hansard, Vol 615, Col 1262. (Ch. 14, 2000)

ANNEX 1

EXISTING LEGISLATION

The Registered Homes Act 1984

Part I

298.   The arrangements provided for under Part I of the Registered Homes Act 1984 apply to residential care homes, defined in section 1 as homes which provide or intend to provide board and personal care for persons who for various reasons, including age and disability, are in need of it. Several exemptions are identified, including hospitals and nursing homes (both NHS and those registered under Part II of the Act), children's homes (as defined in the Children Act 1989) and schools as well as, in certain limited circumstances, homes accommodating no more than three people. The registering authority for residential care homes is defined in section 20 as the local social services authority for the area in which the home is situated.

299.   Sections 4 to 9 set out the requirements and procedures for registration, including payment of a registration fee and an annual fee and the requirement for conditions of registration to be specified on the certificate of registration. Registration is granted unless a ground for refusing registration is made out (section 9). These grounds relate to the fitness of the person, the fitness of the premises and the provision of adequate services. Registration may be cancelled for example, on any grounds which would lead to an application for registration being refused, if an offence against the Act has been committed or if a condition of registration has been breached (section 10). An urgent procedure, requiring application to a magistrate, can be used if there is serious risk to life, health or well-being of the residents in the home (section 11).

300.   Section 12 requires the registering authority to serve a notice on the provider where the authority proposes to:

- grant registration subject to conditions not already agreed with the applicant;
- refuse registration;
- cancel registration (unless this is being sought through the emergency procedure)
- vary an existing condition of registration or impose an additional condition of registration.

301.   In these cases the provider has a right to make representations before the authority finalises its decision (section 13). When the decision is made the provider

has a right of appeal if they are not satisfied. Appeals are heard by the Registered Homes Tribunal (Section 15). The decision will not take effect until the representations and appeal process has been completed. However, if the urgent procedure is used, the home closes immediately and any appeal is heard after the home has closed.

302. Section 16 sets out regulation making powers, section 17 details the Secretary of State's powers of inspection (exercised through the registering authority), and section 18 sets out defences that may be used in proceedings brought under the Act.

Part II

303. Part II of the Act concerns nursing homes and mental nursing homes, the definitions of which are mutually exclusive. The definition of nursing home is very broad, and encompasses any premises where nursing care is provided, from a traditional nursing home for elderly people through to an acute hospital (Section 21). Provision is also made for the Secretary of State to define what are termed 'specially controlled techniques', which at present are class 3b and class 4 lasers. Settings where these techniques are used are also required to register. There are a range of exemptions to this definition, including NHS settings and services provided by local authorities. School sanatoria, first aid rooms, occupational health facilities and facilities to be used solely by a medical or dental practitioner or a chiropodist are also exempt unless specially controlled techniques are in use.

304. Mental nursing homes are separately defined in Section 22, and include any settings where nursing care or treatment is provided for one or more mentally disordered patients. NHS settings and services provided by local authorities are the main exemptions to this definition.

305. The registration procedure is in many respects very similar to that employed under Part I of the Act. Although in this case the Secretary of State formally operates the registration scheme, in practice it is delegated to Health Authorities. Homes may be dually registered under Parts I and II.

306. The key differences between Parts I and II centre on the requirements relating to nursing or medical care in Part II. For example, applicants for mental nursing homes must declare if they wish to take patients detained under the Mental Health Act 1983 (section 23). The person in charge of a nursing or mental nursing home must be a registered medical practitioner, a qualified nurse or a registered midwife in the case of a maternity home, and conditions of registration will include the number of qualified nurses that must be on duty at any time.

307. Procedures relating to variation of registration conditions, cancellation of registration (including an urgent procedure), right to make representations (section 32) and right to appeal (section 34) and inspection powers in nursing homes are very similar to those under Part I. Special provision is made in section 35 for the

inspection of mental nursing homes. This enables a medical practitioner to examine a patient in private and to inspect any medical records relating to that patient's treatment in the home.

Parts III, IV and V

308.   The remaining parts of the Act deal with the Registered Homes Tribunal (Part III), offences (Part IV) and supplementary provisions (Part V).

The Children Act 1989

Fostering

309.   Voluntary organisations which provide accommodation for children are currently regulated under section 59 and 64 of the Children Act 1989, but the position of fostering agencies acting on behalf of local authorities is far less clear. In schedule 2 of the Children Act 1989 (paragraph 12(g)) and subsequent regulations (Foster Placement (Children) Regulations (SI 1991 No 910, regulation 8), local authorities are given powers to delegate the fostering arrangements for any particular child to a voluntary organisation. Agencies recruit and approve prospective foster parents to care for children who are looked after by local authorities, and then provide support for the placement and training for the foster parents whilst the child is placed with them.

Children's Homes

310.   The current system for registering and regulating children's homes is set out in the Children Act 1989. There are three categories of children's home – community homes, defined as those provided directly by local authorities or in partnership with a voluntary organisation or trust; voluntary homes, provided by non-profit making organisations; and registered children's homes, whose providers are private individuals or private sector, rather than local government or voluntary, organisations. These categories of home are dealt with in parts VI, VII and VIII of the Children Act 1989 respectively.

Part VI – Community Homes

311.   Community homes provided by local authorities are called maintained community homes. Community homes provided by voluntary organisations are divided into two further categories (section 53). Where the local authority manages a home provided by a voluntary organisation, the home is designated a controlled community home. Where the voluntary organisation manages the home, it is designated an assisted community home.

312.   No type of community home is registered, but controlled and assisted

community homes are managed in accordance with an instrument of management, which is made by the Secretary of State. In addition to providing the constitution for the body of managers for the home, the instrument may specify the nature and purpose of the home, require a specified proportion of the places to be made available to the local authority or any other named body, and any provision for fees that to be charged. It may also contain any other provisions the Secretary of State considers appropriate. Parts II and III of schedule 4 deal with the management and regulation, of, respectively controlled and assisted community homes.

313. Local authorities make arrangements for inspecting their own community homes. In addition, the Social Services Inspectorate inspect local authority children's services as part of their wider remit to inspect Social Services. Children's residential care is part of those services. When inspecting a local authority's provision they would inspect the community homes maintained by that authority, and an inspection of assisted and controlled community homes might also form part of that wider inspection. As an example, in 1997/8 SSI carried out inspections of 17 local authorities on the theme 'Safety of Children Looked After'.

314. Sections 54-58 contain provisions relating to the closure of controlled and assisted community homes. There are very few of these homes still in existence, and these provisions are very rarely used.

Part VII – voluntary homes and voluntary organisations

315. Part VII deals with voluntary homes and voluntary organisations. Voluntary organisations (such as Barnardo's), may accommodate a child by placing them with family, another suitable person, placing them in a children's home or making other appropriate arrangements. Secretary of State has power to make regulations regarding placements with foster parents and the nature of any alternative arrangements that may be made (Section 59). The current regulations are the Arrangements for Placement of Children (General) Regulations 1991 (SI 1991 No 890) and the Foster Placement (Children) Regulations 1991.

316. Voluntary homes must be registered with the Secretary of State, and are defined, subject to certain exceptions, as homes providing care and accommodation for children which are carried on by a voluntary organisation (Section 60). Schedule 5 details the registration procedure. Secretary of State may grant or refuse registration as he thinks fit, and may grant the application subject to such conditions, as he thinks appropriate. This is in contrast to the approach taken in the Registered Homes Act 1984, whereby registration is granted providing the applicant is a fit person, the premises are suitable and adequate services and facilities will be provided.

317. Section 61 places a duty on a voluntary organisation to safeguard and promote the welfare of any child it arranges or provides accommodation for (though where a local authority with care places a child in a voluntary home, this overarching duty remains with the local authority under section 23). The duty involves making

reasonable use of any services available for children cared for by their own parents and to advise, assist and befriend the child with a view to preparing the child for the time they cease to be looked after by the organisation. Before making any decisions regarding the child, the organisation should take account of the child's wishes and those of their parents and any other person they consider to be relevant.

318. Section 62 lays duties on local authorities regarding any voluntary organisation within its area or any voluntary organisation outside its area providing accommodation for a child on behalf of the authority. The authority has to satisfy itself that the welfare of the children is being safeguarded and promoted, and this includes visiting the child. If the authority is not satisfied, they have a duty to take all reasonable steps to place the child in the care of a parent or relative, so long as this is not contrary to the child's interests, or to consider taking the child into the care of the local authority. The authority has powers of inspection, and it is an offence to obstruct an inspector.

Part VIII – Registered Children's Homes

319. Part VIII concerns privately operated children's homes, ie those not run by a local authority or voluntary organisation. These are homes which accommodate four or more children and which must register with and be inspected by the local authority. They are known as *registered children's homes.* Privately run homes which accommodate fewer than four children ("small children's homes") are not required to register. Section 63 also provides further exemptions including homes registered under the Registered Homes Act 1984 (ie registered care homes, nursing homes and mental nursing homes), NHS settings and most schools. Independent schools are not regarded as children's homes unless they provide accommodation for three or more children for more than 295 days a year.

320. The registration procedure is detailed in Schedule 6. It is very similar to that for voluntary homes, with a few exceptions. The applications for registration are made to the local authority in which the home is situated, and not to the Secretary of State. A registration fee must also be paid. The local authority is required to conduct an annual review of the registration of every registered home. If they are satisfied that the home is being conducted in accordance with its conditions of registration and any other relevant requirements, then the registration is renewed for another year, and an annual fee becomes payable. Should registration be refused or cancelled, the applicant cannot re-apply for a period of six months. Other matters relating to the registration procedure, right to make representations and appeals are identical to those under Part VII.

321. Section 64 concerns the welfare of children in children's homes, and places a duty to safeguard and protect the children's welfare on the person carrying on the home rather than the local authority. Provision is made for section 62 – duties of local authorities, detailed in paragraph 279 above – to apply to registered children's homes

as well as voluntary homes.

Regulations relating to children's homes

322.   The principal instrument governing the conduct of children's homes is the Children's Homes Regulations 1991. Requirements for the conduct of children's homes and the administration of homes apply to all types of home, so despite the variety of categories and registration procedures, the same standards should apply in all settings.

The Adoption Act 1976

323.   The relevant legislation is the Adoption Act 1976 ("the Adoption Act") and the Adoption (Intercountry Aspects) Act 1999 (not yet in force). By section 1 of the Adoption Act, local authorities are placed under a duty to establish and maintain an adoption service for children who have been or who may be adopted; parents and guardians of such children; and persons who have adopted or who may adopt a child. Local authorities may use approved adoption societies to provide this service. In addition, local authorities are under a duty to ensure that their adoption service is provided in conjunction with other local authority social services and services provided by adoption societies in the area. The services provided by local authorities are known as their "adoption service". An adoption agency means a local authority or an approved adoption society.

324.   Section 3 of the Act deals with the approval of adoption societies by the Secretary of State. In addition to considering the standards, qualifications of staff, financial resources etc of the agency, the Secretary of State must also consider whether the agency will make an effective contribution to the adoption service. This provision is effectively a means of controlling the market. Where the agency will operate extensively in the area of a given local authority, he is required to seek the views of that authority and take them into account when considering the application. Approvals are given for three years, after which time the agency has to go through the full application process again.

325.   Approval may be withdrawn if the Secretary of State considers that the agency is no longer making an effective contribution to the Adoption Service (section 4). If the Secretary of State proposes to refuse an application, or withdraw approval, the applicant has the right to make representations but there is no right of appeal against a decision to refuse the application or withdraw approval (section 5).

326.   Section 6 of the Adoption Act places a duty on all adoption agencies, that is, both approved adoption societies and local authorities, to safeguard and promote the welfare of the child, and to take his wishes and feelings into account as far as

possible. This is similar to the duty placed on local authorities under Part III of the Children Act 1989 in respect of children of need and children who are being looked after by the authority. Section 7 requires the agency to take account of the wishes of the child's parent or guardian, so far as possible, regarding the religious upbringing of a child placed for adoption.

327. The conduct of all adoption agencies is regulated by the Adoption Agencies Regulations 1983 (S.I. 1983 No 1964) made under section 9 of the Act. These make provision for the approval of adoption societies and for annual reports and other information to be supplied. They provide for the establishment of adoption panels by adoption agencies and for arrangements to be made by agencies in relation to their adoption work. They specify the procedures to be followed before and after a child is placed for adoption. They make provision for confidentiality and preservation of case records and for access to access to case records and disclosure of information. They also make provision in respect of transfer of case records between adoption agencies and progress reports to former parents of children who have been freed for adoption.

328. The Adoption (Intercountry Aspects) Act 1999 makes provision for intercountry adoption generally and in particular for the ratification of the Hague Convention on the Protection of Children and Cooperation in respect of intercountry Adoption 1993. Section 2(2) makes provision for an approved adoption society to act as an accredited body for the purpose of the Convention.

Legislation relating to Child Minding, Day Care and Nursery Provision

Children Act 1989 Part X and Schedule 9: Child Minding and Day Care for Young Children

329. The current system for the regulation of child minding and day care is set out in Part X and Schedule 9 of the Children Act 1989. Sections 18 and 19 in Part III of the Act confer other duties on local authorities in respect of day care provision.

330. Section 71 of the Act requires local authorities to keep a register of all persons who act as child minders on domestic premises within their area or who provide day care for children under eight within their area. A child minder is defined as a person: who is not a parent or a relative; who looks after one or more children aged under 8 for over 2 hours a day; and who does so for reward. Day care is defined as care, not on domestic premises, which exceeds two hours a day. Day care does not necessarily have to be for reward. Provision is made in Schedule 9 for occasional arrangements to be exempted.

331. Under Sections 72 and 73, a local authority has the power to require providers to meet any reasonable requirements it sets (as appropriate in each particular case) as a condition of registration. Registration may be cancelled under Section 74 if the

circumstances justify it: for example, if the child minder has failed to comply with the registration requirements.

332. Section 75 provides for court orders to be available to cancel or vary a registration. The Court may make the order if it appears to them that a child is suffering or is likely to suffer significant harm. The more standard route is dealt with under Section 77. Fourteen days notice must be given of a refusal or cancellation of registration and provision is made for the person affected to object to the step. Appeal against the decision is to the Magistrate's Court.

333. Under Section 76, a local authority has powers to inspect any domestic premises on which childminding is, at any time, carried out or at which day care is being provided. It may inspect the premises, the children being looked after, the arrangements made for their welfare and any records relating to them which are kept under Part X. The local authority must inspect at least once a year.

334. A person providing day care who contravenes the registration requirement commits an offence (Section 78(1)). A child minder only commits an offence if she continues to act as a child minder without being registered when an enforcement notice has been served on her (Section 78(6)). This gives the local authority some discretion in enforcing the requirements. It is also an offence to fail to comply with the requirements set by the local authority in respect of the registration: for example, exceeding the number of children who may be cared for on the premises.

335. Schedule 9 sets out requirements for applications for registration and the conditions for disqualification from registration. It exempts certain types of school, including a local education authority maintained school, as well as certain other establishments such as a registered children's home. The Schedule also deals with the issue of certificates in respect of registration and for fees chargeable for registration and inspection. There is also a requirement for co-operation between local authorities in the exercise of their functions under Part X.

The legislation governing Nursery Education inspections

336. The inspection of nursery education is governed by Section 122 of the School Standards and Framework Act 1998 and Schedule 26 to that Act.

337. Broadly speaking, any state or state-subsidised provider of nursery education, other than in a nursery school, will be inspected at prescribed intervals by Her Majesty's Chief Inspector Schools. His responsibility is to assess the quality and standards of relevant nursery education and the spiritual moral social and cultural development of children for whom nursery education is provided. He also has a role in advising the Secretary of State more generally with respect to nursery education. The Chief Inspector has no further powers in relation to the provision of such education, he merely reports to the Secretary of State and advises him in relation to

such education.

338.   The inspection requirements do not apply where nursery education is provided at a state school, including a maintained nursery school. These are subject to inspection under the Schools Inspection Act 1996. The application of the inspection regime is, effectively, limited to state sector nursery education and state subsidised nursery education or nursery education which the local authority is considering subsidising.

339.   Under paragraph 6(4) of Schedule 26, provision is made that where an inspection is also due to take place under the Children Act 1989 then the education inspector is to consult with the local authority before undertaking the education inspection.

340.   Under paragraph 8, a register of nursery education inspectors is to be established and maintained.   Only those who the Chief Inspector considers fit and proper persons and competent for the job may be registered. Registration may impose conditions, and a person is only authorised to act as a nursery education inspector in so far as the conditions permit (paragraph 8(7)). Provision is also made under paragraph 8 for removal from the register and variation of the conditions of registration.

Welfare Inspections of Boarding Schools

341.   Under Section 87 of the Children Act 1989, a duty is placed on the proprietor or person in charge of an independent boarding school to safeguard the welfare of the children. A duty is placed on the local authority to satisfy themselves that the welfare of the children is being adequately safeguarded. The authority has a power to inspect at any reasonable time and examine records. Intentional obstruction of an authorised person is an offence. If the authority consider the school is failing in its duty, a report is made to the Secretary of State (for Education and Employment). Sections 87A and 87B were inserted by the Deregulation and Contracting Out Act 1994, and make provision for the appointment of substitute inspectors.

Nurses Agencies Act 1957

342.   The current arrangements for nurses agencies are set out in the Nurses Agencies Act 1957 and associated regulations. In order to operate, agencies have to be licensed. The licensing authority is the County or Borough Council, and in many cases this duty has been delegated to District Councils. The principal requirement regarding conduct of an agency on the face of the 1957 Act is that the selection of each nurse for each placement must be made by, or under the supervision of, a qualified nurse. The Nurses Agencies Regulations 1961 (as amended) set out the classes of nurse that agencies can supply, the form that applications for registration

should take, the records agencies should keep and the registration and annual fees payable.

Regulation of Professional Social Work Training

343.   There are approximately one million people who work in social care. The large majority have no recognised qualifications or training, and there are no nationally agreed standards of practice or conduct. A relatively small number of these million or so workers are employed as *social workers*. The majority of social workers have a professional qualification, which may be the Diploma in Social Work (DipSW), the current qualification, or its predecessors, the Certificate of Social Services and the Certificate of Qualification in Social Work. The training of social workers is currently regulated by the Central Council for Education and Training in Social Work (CCETSW).

344.   CCETSW was originally established under the Health Visiting and Social Work (Training) Act 1962, under the name of "the Council for Training in Social Work". It has undergone two major changes since then, and was established in its present form under section 10 of the Health and Social Services and Social Security Adjudications Act 1983 (the HASSASSA Act).

345.   CCETSW's functions are concerned with training in relevant social work, with some additional functions. 'Relevant social work' is defined in section 10(16) to mean such social work as is required in connection with health, education or social services provided by local authorities, voluntary organisations and certain Northern Ireland bodies, or in connection with the probation service. The functions are set out in section 10(3) of the HASSASSA Act as follows:

> 10 (3) To promote training in relevant social work by:
>
> (a) seeking to secure facilities for training persons in such work,
> (b) approving courses as suitable to be attended by persons engaged, or intending to engage, in such work; and
> (c) seeking to attract persons to such courses.

346.   Approvals for courses are made in accordance with the CCETSW's rules, which are made by CCETSW and approved by the Privy Council. The approval process may include specifying subjects to be included in the course and specifying the conditions for admissions to the courses. Section 10(6)(a) empowers the Council to conduct examinations for approved courses. Section 10(4)(b) gives CCETSW the power to make a professional social work award to students who successfully complete one of the courses it regulates.

347.   If CCETSW considers that the provision of training is inadequate, it has power in section 10(5) to provide or to secure provision of courses for this purpose, although in practice sufficient courses have come forward seeking CCETSW's approval. There

is a further power in section 10(6)(b) to enable the Council to carry out, or assist others in carrying out research into relevant social work training.

348.   In order to attract people to the courses, section 10(7) enables the Council to make grants and pay travelling and other allowances to people resident in Great Britain, to enable them to take up training. This power extends to Great Britain only; the Department of Health and Social Services for Northern Ireland continues to award grants directly to residents of Northern Ireland who undertake social work training.

349.   Section 10(11) enables the Secretary of State to confer additional functions on CCETSW by regulation. This has been exercised once, through the Central Council for Education and Training in Social Work (Functions) Regulations 1991 (SI 1991 No 1123). The effect of these regulations is to extend CCETSW's powers to include responsibility for training in the private sector.

350.   Schedule 3 of the HASSASSA Act sets out the constitution of CCETSW, including membership of the Council, its committees, proceedings, staff, payment of allowances to members and arrangements for accounts and audit. CCETSW is funded by grant-in-aid to cover approved

---

Printed in the UK by The Stationery Office Limited
under the authority and superintendence of Carol Tullo, Controller of
Her Majesty's Stationery Office and Queen's Printer of Acts of Parliament.

1st Impression August 2000
2nd Impression August 2001